THE FAIRY TALE

The Magic Mirror of Imagination

STUDIES IN LITERARY THEMES AND GENRES

Ronald Gottesman, Editor

University of Southern California

THE FAIRY TALE

THE MAGIC MIRROR OF IMAGINATION

Steven Swann Jones

TWAYNE PUBLISHERS
An Imprint of Simon & Schuster Macmillan
New York

Prentice Hall International
London   Mexico City   New Delhi   Singapore   Sydney   Toronto

The Fairy Tale: The Magic Mirror of Imagination
Stephen Swann Jones

Studies in Literary Themes and Genres No. 5

Copyright © 1995 by Simon & Schuster Macmillan

TWAYNE PUBLISHERS
An Imprint of Simon & Schuster Macmillan
1633 Broadway, New York, N.Y. 10019-6785

Library of Congress Cataloging-in-Publication Data

Jones, Stephen. 1949–
    The fairy tale : the magic mirror of imagination / Stephen Swann
Jones.
        p. cm.—(Studies in literary themes and genres ; no. 5)
    Includes bibliographical references (p.   ) and index.
    IBSBN 0-8057-0950-9 (acid-free paper)]
    1. Fairy tales—History and criticism. I. Title. II. Series.
    GR550.J68   1995
398.2—dc20   94-34995
                                                            CIP

10 9 8 7 6 5   (hc)

Printed in the United States of America

For my wife, Rosalyn,
and our sons,
Trent and Tyler

General Editor's Statement

Genre studies have been a central concern of Anglo-American and European literary theory for at least the past quarter century, and the academic interest has been reflected, for example, in new college courses in slave narratives, autobiography, biography, nature writing, and the literature of travel as well as in the rapid expansion of genre theory itself. Genre has also become an indispensable term for trade publishers and the vast readership they serve. Indeed, few general bookstores do not have sections devoted to science fiction, romance, and mystery fiction. Still, genre is among the slipperiest of literary terms, as any examination of genre theories and their histories will suggest.

In conceiving this series we have tried, on the one hand, to avoid the comically pedantic spirit that informs Polonius' recitation of kinds of drama and, on the other hand, the equally unhelpful insistence that every literary production is a unique expression that must not be forced into any system of classification. We have instead developed our list of genres, which range from ancient comedy to the Western, with the conviction that by common consent kinds of literature do exist—not as fixed categories but as fluid ones that change over time as the result of complex interplay of authors, audiences, and literary and cultural institutions. As individual titles in the series demonstrate, the idea of genre offers us provocative ways to study both the continuities and adaptability of literature as a familiar and inexhaustible source of human imagination.

Recognition of the fluid boundaries both within and among genres will provide, we believe, a useful array of perspectives from which to study literature's complex development. Genres, as traditional but open ways of understanding the world, contribute to our capacity to respond to narrative and expressive forms and offer means to discern moral significances embodied in these forms. Genres, in short, serve ethical as well as aesthetic purposes, and the volumes in this series attempt to demonstrate how this double benefit has been achieved as these genres have been transformed over the years. Each title in the series should be measured against this large ambition.

Ron Gottesman

Contents

Chapter 6

Preface

Whether it is the Grimms' version of "Snow White" ("*Schneewittchen*") or Disney's version of *Aladdin,* whether it is a ninth-century Chinese version of "Cinderella" *(Tuan Ch'êng-Shih)* or a seventeenth-century French version of "Beauty and the Beast," whether it is Richard Chase's collection of Appalachian tales or Asbjornsen and Moe's collection of Scandinavian tales, some form of fairy tale has enchanted almost everyone. This study is an attempt to investigate and offer an explanation for the broad appeal of fairy tales.

In order to understand fairy tales, we must begin by exploring their origins in oral tradition. We need to realize to what extent these tales were initially created by storytellers and audiences through the ongoing and evolving process of oral transmission, a process that encourages both *variation* (as a product of the inspiration of storytellers and the contributions of audience members) and *continuity* (as a product of the inherited, traditional forms or structures of the stories). In particular, we need to identify the specific formal characteristics of fairy tales that differentiate them from other oral narratives, such as myths, legends, and folktales.

In addition to familiarizing ourselves with the oral heritage of fairy tales, we need to survey the literary history of this genre. We need to recognize how oral fairy tales were eventually recorded by collectors, shaped by editors, and borrowed by writers for literary audiences all around the world. (And, of course, these traditional fairy tales and their generic characteristics also continue to reappear in other artistic forms, such as films, television, and the performing and visual arts.) The range of examples of fairy tales in literary collections beggars the imagination, because it represents the collective creative input of hundreds of thousands, even millions, of storytellers and writers. And the history is equally overwhelming, the roots of fairy tales going back over hundreds and, in some cases, thousands of years, as an art form quite likely extending back to the dawn of civilization and human intercourse. Storytelling is such a natural form of entertainment, and fictionalized exaggerations of life's experiences are such a common and widespread phenomenon, fairy tales seem as ubiquitous and indigenous as speech itself. For that reason, a thorough survey of the examples and the history of this genre is quite beyond the scope of the present study. It would take an encyclopedia to begin to represent this genre comprehensively. As an introduction to the subject, however, this study will provide, as best it can, a brief overview of the examples and history of the fairy tale as a genre.

Beyond exploring the oral roots and reviewing the literary history of fairy tales, in order to know what fairy tales really are, we need to identify their essential characteristics. Rather than listing every known fairy tale, we need to deduce, from the wide range of examples and ancient history of this genre, what defines the essence of fairy tales—what are their main characteristics.

Certainly, other scholars have previously endeavored to explore and account for fairy tales, and part of the goal of this study will be to review their contributions as well (see the Bibliographic Essay). Bruno Bettelheim is perhaps the scholar best known for exploring fairy tales' uses of enchantment, although there are quite a number of important scholars (such as Sigmund Freud, Carl Jung, and Joseph Campbell) whose work preceded his and to whom Bettelheim is indebted for premises and insights. These psychological interpretations show how the content of fairy tales might be seen as reflecting in an exaggerated and symbolic way the personal concerns of audience members, which constitutes one major explanation of the appeal of these stories.

Of course, delving into the emotional underworld of audiences is always a murky task at best, and readers must indeed reserve a certain skepticism in reviewing past and present psychological analyses. But they should not discount entirely the notion that fairy tales appeal to audiences through their emotions. The stories survive because we *like* them or *love* them, and if the insights offered by the psychological approach do not seem accurate or adequate enough to account for the popularity of these tales, then it is incumbent upon students of this genre to find some other explanations that more effectively account for its existence and popularity.

Other scholars have, in fact, tried to account for fairy tales in ways apart from the psychological approach. Jack Zipes, Lutz Röhrich, Linda Dégh, and others have taken a sociohistorical perspective, connecting the tales to the social realities of the lives of specific ethnic communities. Within the sociohistorical approach, we can find various specific orientations, such as a neo-Marxist perspective that sees the tales perpetuating a bourgeois mentality, or a feminist perspective that sees the tales promulgating sexist dogma (see, for example, Sandra Gilbert's analysis). The relevant context for these scholars is not so much the personal one of the family structure and the subliminal fears and desires of individual audience members, as it is the social context of cultural codes and norms, of the inscription of cultural values and the socialization of audiences. They have shown how fairy tales operate as cultural primers and mirrors, revealing another important function that helps to explain their existence.

In addition to the psychological and sociohistorical approaches, we have formalist approaches such as structuralism and narratology (as practiced by scholars such as Vladimir Propp, Alan Dundes, and Heda Jason), which attempt to analyze fairy tales from the point of view of their characteristic form or style. Max Lüthi's contributions are particularly useful in this regard, as he attempts to delineate what he calls the abstract style of fairy tales. The aesthetic and philosophical function of fairy tales to provide a sense of order, beauty, and meaning in the world is revealed as another basis for their appeal to audiences.

At times, the insights generated by these various approaches are almost as fascinating as the tales themselves, and they do help to explain the mysterious appeal of fairy tales. Making sense of all these approaches to fairy tales, however, while simultaneously trying to maintain a sense of the great corpus of fairy tales, is no small task. If this study can help readers accomplish this goal, then it may have some value on that score alone.

Ultimately, however, this study proposes to build upon the insights offered by previous scholars and their various approaches in order to identify the major characteristics of fairy tales and account for their popularity. This study deduces from the rhetoric, images, plots, and themes employed in fairy tales a nucleus of essential characteristics that typify these tales. These primary characteristics include: the use of fantasy; the confronting of a problem; the successful resolution of that problem; the use of a sympathetic protagonist; and the presence of a thematic core. Evidence of this nucleus is then examined in four traditional fairy tales and three literary fairy tales. To the extent that the specific tales illustrate the characteristics identified as typifying fairy tales, this study should be of value in helping readers to understand the genre and its basic appeal to audiences. While identifying such a "key" to all fairy tales is admittedly an ambitious undertaking, it is my hope that this study offers one reasonably comprehensible and illuminating perspective on the intriguing, enchanting, and ever disingenuous realm of fairy tales.

Finally, I would like to thank those who helped to make this book possible: my wife, Rosalyn, for her help and encouragement; my parents, Curtis and Elizabeth Jones, for their support and careful reading of the manuscript; my sons, Trent and Tyler, for their patience in sitting at my feet as I wrote; California State University, Los Angeles, for providing the time and resources that enabled me to undertake the research; and my editors, Ron Gottesman of the University of Southern California and Sylvia K. Miller of Twayne Publishers, for their valuable suggestions and guidance.

Chronology

Obviously, with a genre that is to a large extent prehistoric in origin, a chronology can represent only the record of the appearance of this genre in print. As chapter 3 documents, various classic collections appeared in manuscript form during the Middle Ages in India, the Middle East, the Mediterranean area, and Europe, and they included fairy tales as part of their recording and reworking of the oral traditions of those cultures. After the Renaissance, we begin to have a more precise chronology of the evolution of the fairy tale in literary tradition.

14th century	Boccaccio, *Decameron.*
16th century	Straparola, *The Pleasant Nights.*
1634	Basile, *Pentamerone.*
1697	Perrault, *Contes du Ma Mère L'Oye.*
1729	Perrault, *Tales of Mother Goose* (first English translation).
1744	Newbery, *A Little Pretty Pocketbook.*
1782	Musäus, *Volksmärchen der Deutschen.*
1785–1789	*Le Cabinet des Fees* (42 vols.), in which appeared Mme de Villeneuve's version of *Beauty and the Beast,* among other fairy tales.

1893 Jacobs, *More English Fairy Tales*.

1900 Bannerman, *Little Black Sambo*.

1900 Baum, *The Wizard of Oz*.

1904 Barrie, *Peter Pan* (produced as a play; retold in narrative form in 1911 under the title *Peter and Wendy*).

1910 de la Mare, *The Three Royal Monkeys*.

1919 MacManus, *Donegal Fairy Stories*.

1920 Lofting, *The Story of Dr. Dolittle*.

1926 Milne, *Winnie-the-Pooh*.

1934 Travers, *Mary Poppins*.

1937 Tolkien, *The Hobbit*.

1939 T. H. White, *The Once and Future King*.

1943 Chase, *The Jack Tales*.

1943 Saint-Exupéry, *The Little Prince*.

1950 Lewis, *The Lion, the Witch, and the Wardrobe*.

1952 Norton, *The Borrowers*.

1952 E. B. White, *Charlotte's Web*.

1957 Seuss, *The Cat in the Hat*.

1962 L'Engle, *A Wrinkle in Time*.

1963 Sendak, *Where the Wild Things Are*.

1

The Folklore Origin and the Definition of the Fairy Tale

One of the most well-known, most loved, and most influential genres of literature is the fairy tale. Since it was originally a product of oral tradition, this genre dates back, not just to the Middle Ages or biblical times, but to well before recorded history itself. Oral literature inevitably precedes written culture, and the earliest written records in almost every culture acknowledge the preexistence of fairy tales. In addition to its oral popularity, the fairy tale genre has enthralled millions of readers through numerous published collections of folklore—such as those produced by the Grimms and Andrew Lang—as well through its cultivation by literary notables such as Hans Christian Andersen, Charles Dickens, John Ruskin, William Makepeace Thackeray, Oscar Wilde, and L. Frank Baum. This long and diverse heritage makes the task of defining the genre difficult, especially in light of its dual existence in folklore and belles lettres.

In order to define the fairy tale genre, we must first identify the preliterate heritage from which these tales emerged. We need to understand the process of oral narration and the characteristics of oral transmission in order to understand why fairy tales as one kind of folk narrative take the form they do. Second, we need to review previous attempts to classify and catalog the multitudinous products of oral tradition. For over a century, folklorists have tried to differentiate and to index the various forms of folk narrative, including fairy tales, so we need to build on their findings. Third, from this theoretical foundation, we may begin to deduce what are the essential qualities characterizing the genre. Part of this task involves differentiating fairy tales from related genres such as myths and legends. Ultimately, we may then use this folkloristic definition of the fairy tale to identify literary examples that emulate or imitate the folklore model.

The Preliterate Heritage

To understand the heritage of the fairy tale fully, we must first recognize the mechanics of oral transmission—the ability of people to create and retell stories without the aid of books. The majority of the world's best-known and most loved fairy tales, including "Snow White," "Jack and the Beanstalk," "Sleeping Beauty," and "Cinderella," were all initially the product of folklore. The importance of folklore in our literate society is underestimated, however, perhaps because the very concept of folklore is not well understood. We tend to be condescending toward traditional culture and to think of it as represented primarily by the quaint costumes and peculiar customs of backward people. But folklore includes all the forms of cultural learning passed on by word of mouth or personal example in any group. Folklore flourishes in preindustrial, industrial, and "postindustrial" societies—not only along the Congo or the Amazon. Folklore includes all the traditional forms of expression that circulate without the aid of books—the art, speech, and literature created through personal interaction rather than through the printed medium. Rap music, for example, has a large oral component, as it is performed and perpetuated on the sidewalks of New York and other cities, and it may be seen as an outgrowth of the folk tradition of "toasting" as it was performed in African-American culture. Likewise, quilting continues to be a popular art form passed on by personal example from parent to child, neighbor to friend, in farming communities all across America. Much like these other art forms, jokes continue to flourish as an oral tradition in all walks of life—young and old pass on jokes they have heard from others. And, of course, a host of fairy tales, such as "East o' the Sun, West o' the Moon" (also known in its literary versions as "Beauty and the Beast" or "Cupid and Psyche"), "Aladdin's Lamp," "The Spirit in the Blue Light" (also known in its literary version as "The Tinder Box"), "The Dragon Slayer," "The Shoes That Were Danced to Pieces," "Little Red Riding Hood," "Hans the Hedgehog," "Rapunzel," "Rumplestiltskin," and "The Frog King," owe their existence to folk tradition.

Because of its folkloric heritage, there are some special problems in defining an originally oral genre such as the fairy tale. First of all, since the tales circulated orally at the start, there are no exact and established versions, no identifiable authors, and no fixed titles. In oral tradition, fairy tales circulate over hundreds and, in some cases, thousands of years in multiple versions, adapted by different narrators in a style or manner specific to each narrator, often in very different historical circumstances. What we have are many versions of the same story coming not only from different narrators, but from different societies and cultures. There are collections of fairy tales from almost every culture. In short, fairy tales are a variegated and ever-varying phenomenon.

With so much diversity associated with folk fairy tales, it would seem a problematic, if not impossible, task to define this genre precisely. However, underlying the apparent fluidity of the texts is their surprisingly strict adherence to some basic structures characterizing the genre. In other words, despite superficial variations, we can discern *significant formal continuities* that suggest these texts do indeed belong to a shared genre. From a theoretical perspective, however, our ability to identify these formal continuities is predicated on our ability to determine the conformance of specific collected texts to what folklorists refer as "tale types."

A tale type is a term coined by folklorists to describe a basic story, such as "Snow White," that is told in different ways in oral tradition. The individual versions would more closely parallel our conception of a single literary tale, inasmuch as they have

3

individual authors, even if these are anonymous. However, in oral tradition there are a great many individual versions of what is essentially a single story. There is no such thing as plagiarism in oral tradition. For example, there are over four hundred collected versions of "Snow White," ranging over five hundred years. Accordingly, "Snow White" cannot be defined by any single version, since in theory they are all equally legitimate.

Instead, a fairy tale is defined as the sum of its versions. *From the coinciding events or episodes in texts that apparently tell the same basic story, a plot outline for that tale is deduced.* That plot outline is used to define that fairy tale, which is considered a discrete tale type. Other collected texts that follow the same specified sequence of episodes typical of that tale type are considered versions of it. For example, in the case of "Snow White," narratives that relate how a young girl is the victim of jealousy in her home, is expelled and adopted by some companions, is attacked and killed by her rival, and is exhibited and finally resuscitated and married, would be said to be versions of that tale type. There are surprisingly large numbers of texts collected from oral tradition that do indeed conform to one or another of these recognizable tale types, that present a basic sequence of distinctive events characteristic of an established tale type. (In contrast, many of the stylistic features—or motifs—of the tales, which include the characters, settings, objects, and other descriptive details as well as the rhetorical formulas, can and do reappear in a variety of tale types; in other words, these motifs have a life of their own separate from a specific fairy tale.) In sum, the plot outline is regarded as the defining feature of specific tales, and the different versions of these tales that follow the same plot outline are believed to be a product of oral transmission, since coincidental creation of such a specific plot outline is highly unlikely.

The fact that a particular tale type is appealing and popular enough to encourage storytellers to repeat it over centuries and across national boundaries in a recognizably similar form shows us the remarkable stability of the narrative, especially in light of the fluid nature of oral transmission, where conceivably each narrator could dramatically alter any story he or she related. The stability reveals, moreover, the underlying appeal and significance of that narrative for its audiences. The fact that it has been remembered and repeated demonstrates that it has touched people's lives. It has been deemed worthy of repetition because it is loved, and it is loved because it tells us something about ourselves that we want and need to know. In other words, there is a connection between the long-standing and far-reaching popularity of a fairy tale like "Snow White" and its subject matter.

Fairy tales, then, are narratives that have been shaped over centuries of retelling and that have achieved a basic narrative form that is a distillation of human experience. Their popularity is a confirmation not only of their aesthetic appeal, but also of their ability to speak to the human heart. This enduring emotional appeal is confirmed by the fact that these jewels of artistic expression have been retold by generations of taletellers and treasured by generations of readers, and have continued to resurface in television and film, like the parody of "Little Red Riding Hood" that popped up in a 1993 episode of the television series "Northern Exposure," where a central character has a dream in which she is lured off the path by a wolfish man articulating a Freudian interpretation of the tale, convincing her to overcome her childish oedipal attachment. Other examples include the retelling of more than a dozen fairy tales in Shelley Duvall's well-received *Fairy Tale Theater,* or the enormously popular animated versions of *Snow White, Cinderella, Beauty and the Beast,* and *Aladdin* produced by Disney. The fairy tales identified above are classics because audiences of all sorts (oral, literary, dramatic, cinematographic, audiovisual) have cherished them. As an example, it is no surprise that "Cinderella" is so well liked in literary and cinematographic forms; more than 500 versions of it have been collected from oral tradition. In sum, the evidence of the multiple versions of fairy tale types in oral tradition is not only a way to define these stories, it is a confirmation of the central appeal and importance of the fairy tale genre.

Where these traditional stories came from will always be a mystery. Most likely they evolved from a prototypical form into their recognizable form over hundreds, if not thousands, of years and through the contributions of thousands, if not millions, of taletellers. But one or more of them could also have been the product of a single creative act by an inspired storyteller, which was in turn remembered and repeated by others. Still, the process is so spontaneous and ahistorical—in the sense that the tales are intrinsically removed from any written record—that we will never know with certainty who created them. The Grimms did not invent "Snow White," nor did the seven informants from whom they collected versions of this narrative.[1] They simply published one somewhat edited and modified version that became extremely popular in the literary world. As a matter of fact, the Italian author Giovanni Batiste Basile had published a version some 300 years previously, but he also had not invented it.[2] The credit for the invention of that tale, and of most of the classic fairy tales, goes to folk tradition, to the heritage of story-tellers who borrowed, altered, and retold in multiple versions tales that their audiences found enjoyable. (See Bengt Holbek's *Interpretation of Fairy Tales* for an extended discussion of one exemplary teller of fairy tales, Evald Tang Kristensen.)[3] From this heritage, many authors and collectors have culled wonderful stories that modern audiences continue to enjoy.

The Classification and Cataloging of Fairy Tales

Having acquired a sense of the mechanics of oral transmission and an awareness of the underlying stability and continuity of folk narratives, we may now move to our second goal: reviewing previous attempts at classifying and cataloging the numerous products of oral tradition that apparently conform to the genre of the fairy tale. Rather than working from a theoretical definition of the genre against which various texts were measured, the earliest attempts to classify fairy tales simply worked inductively, by listing other versions and tales that seemed to resemble the known tales (primarily those in the Grimms' collection) that had been popularly called fairy tales (or *Märchen* in German).

In the early nineteenth century, Johannes Bolte and George Polívka initiated the process of classifying fairy tales by referencing as many parallel versions as they could find for the 210 popular narratives published in the Grimms' collection of fairy tales between 1812 and 1815.[4] Following their lead, Antti Aarne used the Grimms' collection as the basis for a preliminary catalog for folktales: he expanded the list of known variants for the Grimms' tales and identified other fairy tales as well.[5] Stith Thompson significantly enlarged and revised Aarne's index to produce a jointly authored work entitled *The Types of the Folktale*.[6] In it, Aarne and Thompson identify the essential episodes, which they call "action traits," of the major folk fairy tales and list many of the collected versions for each tale. Fairy tales are listed as "Tales of Magic" in *The Types of the Folktale* and are assigned tale type numbers 300–749. (Other classifications include: Animal Tales, 1–299; Supernatural and Religious Tales, 700–849; Romantic Tales, 850–999; Stupid Ogre Tales, 1000–1199; Jokes and Anecdotes, 1200–1999; and Formula Tales, 2000–2399.)

A brief outline of the main episodes is given for each tale type. From the synopsis of main events we can determine if a given text is a version of one of the traditionally popular fairy tales. For example, we can see that Hans Christian Andersen's tale of "The Tinder Box" is actually a retelling of the traditional fairy tale "The Spirit in the Blue Light" (referred to as AT 562, which corresponds to the number assigned to this tale type in Aarne and Thompson's index).[7] Thompson's companion text, *The Folktale*, provides useful and more readable summaries of almost every significant folk fairy tale circulating in Europe.[8] These basic resources are crucial to an appreciation of the vital folkloric heritage of fairy tales. From them we can identify a wide variety of popular fairy tales that have entertained audiences for hundreds of years.

Identifying the Essential Qualities of the Fairy Tale

This comparative approach to fairy tales is an important starting point for defining the genre, for it allows us to differentiate folk fairy tales from those that are the product of the individual imagination of literary authors, and to see which of the literary productions are able to duplicate the charm and the appeal of the traditional favorites. The comparative approach also affords us a perspective on the different versions that reveals continuities within the tale types. What we find is that while individual versions may *vary their motifs* (the stylistic details used to relate the events), they are quite consistent in their *adherence to the plot outline* (that is, the sequence of basic episodes) of the tale type. It is as if they have an underlying narrative backbone or outline that they follow. (For further analysis of this narrative structure of fairy tales, see my 1990 study, *The New Comparative Method*.)

This narrative consistency extends, moreover, to their adherence to generic qualities. *Not only do individual versions follow with remarkable regularity the traditional story line of one established tale type or another, they adhere to the basic characteristics of the genre with equal regularity.* Perhaps the salient characteristics of the fairy tale genre can initially be recognized most easily by differentiating them from the characteristics of other related folk narratives. Folklore scholars generally recognize three major forms of folk narrative: myth, legend, and folktale. Myths are etiological narratives that use *gods* (divine, immortal figures) to explain the operation and purpose of the cosmos. Legends are quasi-historical narratives that use *exceptional and extraordinary protagonists* and depict remarkable phenomena to illustrate cultural ideals, values, and norms. Finally, folktales are entertaining narratives that use *common, ordinary people* as protagonists to reveal the desires and foibles of human nature. The following outline illustrates the relationship of fairy tales to other folk narratives:

Folk Narratives

I. Myths—etiological narratives employing immortal protagonists

II. Legends—quasi-historical narratives employing extraordinary protagonists

III. Folktales—quotidian narratives employing ordinary protagonists
   A. Fables—didactic or moralistic tales
   B. Jokes—humorous tales
   C. Novellas—romantic tales
   D. Fairy Tales—magical tales

This elementary distinction between the primary characters of these different oral narratives has broad implications for these disparate genres. The way we relate to a story about an immortal protagonist is quite different from the way we relate to one about a mortal figure. Similarly, we identify differently with an extraordinary individual than we do with an ordinary figure.

Immortal protagonists are linked with the immutable laws of the cosmos; their situations and actions illustrate cosmogonic and paradigmatic principles. When a god rebels against his father, he is exemplifying the universal pattern of each successive generation supplanting the previous one. Consequently, audiences relate to myths as sacred and esoteric texts.

Extraordinary heroes are the embodiments of their culture; they are larger than typical figures in ordinary life (often literally so) because they are exemplars of their society's aspirations and sociopolitical conflicts. When a legendary hero dies (such as Sigurd, El Cid, Roland), he illustrates not just his own personal weaknesses, but the failings of society at large. As a result, legends serve as social guidelines for behavior and are regarded as having a certain historical and cultural truth embodied in them.

Finally, the ordinary protagonists of folktales remind us of ourselves, and their quests and questions are on a very personal level the same as ours. Their concerns with getting married and establishing a home speak directly to our most individual needs. As a result, we regard folktales as personal entertainment, as engaging fictions reflecting our ability to laugh at ourselves as well as to express our deepest dreams and fears.

Within this last category of folktales, we can identify a variety of genres. Fairy tales are considered one genre of the folktale, since they, like other genres of the folktale, employ ordinary protagonists to address issues of everyday life. There is an important distinction, however, between the fairy tale and the other genres of the folktale, such as the romantic tale, the humorous tale or joke, and the cautionary tale or fable. This essential distinction forms the fundamental basis for the identification of the genre of the fairy tale. While these other genres of the folktale are reasonably mimetic—that is, they depict life in fairly realistic terms— *fairy tales depict magical or marvelous events or phenomena as a valid part of human experience.* The very name of the genre is drawn from this essential characteristic: they are fairy tales because they depict the wondrous magic of the fairy realm. We should not, however, interpret the name too literally. Even if they have no fairies in them, stories that depict the world of magical fantasy are still referred to as fairy tales. Since, in the English folk tradition, the fairy realm is the embodiment of the magical aspect of the world, its name is used metonymically to refer to all folktales that incorporate the magical and the marvelous. In England they are also referred to as wonder tales, a term that more generically references the tale's essential focus on fantastic events and characters.

Two other genres of folktale are also apparently nonrealistic in their presentation—animal fables and tall tales. Animal fables, however, such as the well-known Bre'r Rabbit, use personified animals to depict otherwise realistic human behavior. The personification is seen purely as a literary device for isolating and portraying human foibles, not as an ontologically or philosophically accurate representation of the phenomenal world.

Similarly, in the tall tale, the marvelous events are considered artistic exaggerations, storytelling "lies" for the entertainment of the audience, and part of the point of the story is to stretch credibility beyond the breaking point for humorous effect. In a tall tale such as "The Lucky Shot" (AT 1890), where a single shot kills an unbelievable amount of game, the fantastic phenomena are not ultimately to be believed, whereas in the fairy tale we are expected to accept these magical elements in the narratives at face value, as truly and legitimately occurring in the stories. The attitude of the fairy tale toward this fairy magic is one of awe and supernatural acceptance of powers greater than ourselves. Unlike the tall tale, which foregrounds human rationality and treats the wondrous phenomena described by the storyteller as whimsical artifice, the fairy tale suggests that magic of the fairy realm is not to be taken lightly, but rather to be regarded with respect and even some trepidation.

Thus, just as we can differentiate folktales from other forms of folk narrative by their use of ordinary protagonists, we can differentiate the genre of the fairy tale from other forms of the folktale by its incorporation of and attitude toward magic and fantasy. Scholars such as Axel Olrik, Max Lüthi, and Bruno Bettelheim concur with the designation of fantasy as one of the essential characteristics of the fairy tale.[9] In contrast to the realism of other forms of folktale or literary expression, fairy tales are dominated by fantasy; they involve significant interactions with the magical and the marvelous. The magical dimension is presented earnestly and figures prominently in the protagonist's experiences. Whether it is a talking mirror, a talking horse, a magic cloak, or a magic lamp, the story must include the protagonist's interaction with something magical, an interaction that serves to validate the existence of things magical in this world. Whether it entails cutting off of the multiple heads of some loathsome creature, as in "The Dragon-Slayer" (AT 300), benefiting from a talking cat's advice, as in "The Cat as Helper" (AT 545), or sleeping with a talking frog, as in "The Frog King" (AT 440), fairy tales invoke the fantastic.

The function or meaning of the fantasy in fairy tales is related to its generic characteristic of addressing issues of everyday life, of dramatizing the desires and foibles of human nature. One essential characteristic of the fairy tale is that it presents these quotidian concerns in nonmimetic ways. In other words, fairy tales use the poetic and exaggerated symbolism of fantasy to represent the deep-seated feelings of ordinary individuals in facing the typical challenges of life. As Freud, Jung, Géza, Róheim, Lüthi, Erich Fromm, Joseph Campbell, Bettelheim, and a host of others have suggested, fairy tales speak the language of the unconscious mind. In other words, the fantastic creations in fairy tales may be seen as metaphoric dramatizations of the thoughts and feelings audience members may harbor about their daily lives and the problems they face.[10] These metaphoric dramatizations are expressed in the symbolism of the unconscious mind, in the language of dreams, so to speak. One function of and raison d'être for fairy tales, then, is to give expression to unconscious fears and desires. Given the hypothesis that we possess such a subliminal dimension in our psyche, we should not be surprised that it should find expression in literature and that its form in literature should resemble its manifestations in our dreams. Part of the charm and power of fairy tales, therefore, is their ability to tap into and give vent to this hidden and volatile source of emotional energy.

If we accept the existence of the unconscious and see fantasy as an expression of it, then it seems reasonable to conclude that the occurrence of fantasy in fairy tales proceeds in part from the epistemological difference between the conscious and unconscious minds. In other words, the conscious mind and the unconscious understand the world differently. While the conscious mind may be said to be rationally and logically based, deriving its understanding of the world from and in turn conceptualizing the world by empirical observation and mimetic assessment, the unconscious mind is apparently nonrationally and analogically based, operating through metaphor and association. The term "analogical" is used not only to suggest the opposition of this way of viewing the world to rational logic (it is *non*logical), but also to indicate that the essential characteristic of this perspective is its reliance on analogy, on the heuristic techniques of metaphoric and symbolic conceptualization and association. At the heart of the fairy tale is the representation of the world (both internally, the world of the individual psyche, and externally, the world of society and the cosmos) through the poetic devices of exaggeration, metonymy, simile, and metaphor. Central to the justification of this perspective is the subjective nature of perception itself: how things appear is a matter of how we see them or want to see them, and thus this nonliteral, nonobjective representation may actually be, in its own way, a valid representation of our relationship to the feelings inside us and the people and world around us.

The incorporation of fantasy may be regarded as the most salient formal or stylistic feature of this genre. Max Lüthi's extensive stylistic analysis of the fairy tale (he has devoted at least three books and numerous articles to this subject) could be said to boil down to this essential point: fairy tales are dominated by the fantastic perspective, which is a product of the unconscious, intuitive, and imaginative aspects of the mind.[11] He calls it the abstract style of fairy tales, their propensity for essentializing things and depicting them in vivid ways, but in *The European Folktale* (94–95) he ultimately links this abstract style to the fantastic orientation of the unconscious mind. The style or form of the fairy tale genre thus may be said to be a product of its epistemology, and the epistemology of fairy tales may be summed up in the words of Antoine de St. Exupéry: "It is only with the heart that one can see rightly; what is essential is invisible to the eye."[12] Even this statement employs the technique of metaphoric description: the heart stands for the part of us that sees the world emotionally, instinctively, and subjectively. The heart itself does not see, but the image effectively conveys the epistemological message that the feeling-based perspective of the unconscious mind is a more authentic reading of the world than the factually based cataloging of scientific empiricism. In sum, in its use of fantasy, the fairy tale may be said to be both depicting the unconscious thoughts and feelings residing in the psyche of its audiences, and using the style and semiotics (the linguistic symbols and form of language) of the unconscious mind itself to do it.

Another explanation for the manifestation of fantasy in fairy tales might be that they are affirming a spiritual perspective on the world, much like myths. The belief in the existence of wonder and miracles in the world is the foundation of religious faith, the idea that the numinous or divine realm is in some way manifested in the mundane realm of quotidian life. And fairy tales, through their incorporation of fantasy, inherently promulgate a belief in things unseen, a testament to the existence of another dimension to our existence. This magical element is depicted as generally unobserved or undervalued by most people, however; either they do not see the magic—as is the case in "Aladdin's Lamp" (AT 561), where the lamp is hidden in a cave and appears rusty and old, or in "Cinderella" (AT 510), where the fairy godmother appears only to the heroine—or they do not properly appreciate the magic, as in "The Old Fisherman and His Wife" (AT 555), where the magic wishes are misused, or in "The Table, the Ass, and the Stick" (AT 563), where the magic items are stolen for personal profit. This depiction of the magic suggests the fairy tale's criticism of the materialism and neglect of spiritual values in contemporary society. The spiritual perspective needs to be recovered and polished up to be appreciated, and then it can work wonders for the protagonist.

Furthermore, generally this magical element in fairy tales serves to underscore and affirm a moral propriety in the universe, documenting a cosmic morality, if you will. When the magical agents come to the rescue or assistance of the protagonist—as, for example, in "Cinderella" when a fairy godmother magically provides the means to attend the ball or in "The Kind and Unkind Girls" (AT 480), where the supernatural figure covers the heroine with a shower of gold—we are seeing the affirmation of the cosmic morality. These protagonists are rewarded because they are inherently good and deserve to be rewarded, and the supernatural help serves as a confirmation that the world is indeed a moral one. Similarly, the fantastic forces and acts in fairy tales frequently serve to punish the evil characters—as, for example, when Cinderella's stepsisters' eyes are pecked out by the birds or the unkind stepsister in "The Kind and Unkind Girls" is covered by a shower of dung or pitch by the supernatural agent. Thus, the magical fantasy of fairy tales asserts a twofold philosophical vision, affirming the existence of a metaphysical and mystical dimension of the universe, which is at times Christian and other times generic supernaturalism, as well as asserting a belief in the moral propriety upheld by this metaphysical dimension of the universe and instructing the audience how to conform to it. This moral propriety, as we will see in the next chapter, is itself a product of traditional, and generally patriarchal, cultural values.

Beyond the inclusion of the fantastic, there are a number of typical, if not necessary, characteristics of this genre. For example, various scholars, such as Lüthi, Campbell, Bettelheim, and Vladimir Propp have identified *the confronting and resolving of a problem, frequently by the undertaking of a quest, as essential to the fairy tale*.[13] Admittedly, this is a characteristic shared by other genres as well; for example, heroic legends, one of the subgenres within the category of legend, frequently depict their protagonists as engaging in a quest, such as Odysseus, Perseus, Theseus, Jason, Sigurd, and Beowulf. While there is a distinct correlation between heroic legends and many fairy tales in their plot structure, there are also some differences as well. The protagonists of heroic legends are not only extraordinary (as opposed to the ordinary characters of fairy tales), but their mission is generally directed at an objective to benefit their people (Beowulf attempting to stop the rampaging of Grendel, Odysseus trying to bring his crew back home, Theseus trying to stop the sacrificing of his country's young people, Jason restoring the golden fleece to his community), while the protagonists of fairy tales seek to improve their own lot (marrying the princess or the prince for themselves or acquiring a kingdom for themselves).

Some scholars, for example, Propp and Campbell, have attempted to define more specifically the elements and goals of this quest in the fairy tale. For example, in *Morphology of the Folktale* (by which Propp meant the fairy tale or wonder tale; see *Theory and History of Folklore*), Propp attempts to identify a sequential pattern of 31 elements of the fairy tale's plot structure, some of which refer to the undertaking of a quest.[14] There are a number of problems with Propp's structural definition of the fairy tale genre. His elements are too general, such that his structure can be applied to any narrative, not just fairy tales. For example, Propp identifies "Lack" and "Villainy" as elements (or "functions," to use Propp's term) of a basic fairy tale plot. What story does not have these elements? Furthermore, this pattern of functions does not describe individual tales with a sufficient degree of specificity or rigor. Since, according to Propp, tales may incorporate only a few of these 31 functions, two tales may have entirely different combinations of these elements in them, which does not exactly constitute a valid basis for structural equivalence. Thus, Propp's structural model is overly ambitious. While Propp's observation that many fairy tales depict quests to resolve problems is valid, his attempt to subsume that plot as well as other nonquest plots such as "The Fisherman and His Wife" (AT 555) and "Rapunzel" (AT 310) into one Ur-plot is self-defeating.

Joseph Campbell, in *The Hero with a Thousand Faces*, also identifies a quest pattern as typifying fairy tales, but he does not try to define the fairy tale genre by it. Rather, he links the appearance of this pattern in *some* fairy tales with its use in other forms of literature and art—for example, myths, religious narratives, legends, and ritual ceremonies. His paradigm follows the ideas of Arnold van Gennep and Carl Jung (and is echoed by Victor Turner in *The Ritual Process*), and it identifies a pattern of separation (call to adventure, threshold crossing), initiation (confrontation with antagonist, divinity), and return (return crossing and reincorporation into the community).[15]

Of particular relevance to our discussion of fairy tales is Campbell's assessment that the threshold crossing involves a crossing into another realm, a realm of magic and fantasy. This observation ties in with the first essential characteristic of the fairy tale identified above, the appearance of the marvelous. Campbell's model illuminates the relationship of the fantastic and the quotidian in fairy tales: they are perceived as coexisting in tangential worlds that the protagonist experiences and must reconcile. Campbell's analysis suggests a possible interpretation of the significance of the fantastic in fairy tales. Inasmuch as the protagonist undertakes a journey to experience this magical aspect—for example, the heroine of "The Kind and Unkind Girls" falls down a well and encounters a talking tree that asks her to remove its apples and a stove that asks her to remove its bread—Campbell argues that the occurrence of the fantasy in the fairy tales represents in part the protagonist's exploration of his or her own unconscious mind. The threshold crossing is, in this light, a crossing from the conscious, rational realm to a fictional representation of the unconscious, nonrational domain of the individual's psyche. The fantastic or marvelous element in fairy tales, thus, may be seen as a fictional dramatization of the contents and perspective of the unconscious mind. This theory provides a connection between a typical structural pattern in fairy tales and their fundamental incorporation of the fantastic as a mode of expression. Not only does the fantasy in fairy tales symbolically give expression to the unconscious feelings and thoughts of audience members, but the adventurous quest into an essentially fantastic world frequently undertaken by fairy tale protagonists refers to the corresponding experience of exploring what lurks beneath the tenuous veil of our own conscious and rational minds: for example, the hero in "The Danced-Out Shoes" (AT 306), with the aid of a magic cloak that makes him invisible, follows the princesses through a secret opening under one of the beds to a magical kingdom, where they dance their shoes to pieces.

Furthermore, we may use Campbell's assessment of the kind of initiation experienced by the protagonist, as well as the nature of the objective of the quest, to differentiate between the quests of fairy tales and those of myths or legends. The objective of the mythic quest is oneness with the divine, and accordingly the initiation is a spiritual one in myths, an apotheosis or spiritual awakening. The objective of the legendary quest is social harmony, the overcoming of social problems and the defeat of cultural adversaries, and accordingly the initiation is into the cultural ideals of behavior. The objective of the fairy tale quest is personal happiness, measured as a rule by domestic satisfaction and tranquility. The emphasis is on personal relationships to family members and mates, and the initiation is into a greater awareness of one's own desires and fears. While these kinds of initiations are not the exclusive property of the respective genres that typically illustrate them—myths also depict initiations into social and personal awareness, just as legends depict cosmic and individual lessons, and fairy tales offer insights into cosmic and cultural principles—we can discern a recognizable emphasis in each genre: whereas the focus in myths and legends seems to be on cosmic and cultural lessons, respectively, the focus of fairy tales is apparently on journeys of self-discovery, recognition and confrontation of internal anxieties and desires.

The successful solving of a dilemma facing the protagonist is essential to the plot of the fairy tale. *This happy ending is such a basic and important aspect of the genre, it may be regarded as a third definitional feature.* Whereas myths and legends sometimes end tragically, such as with Baldar's death or Sigurd's death, fairy tales always reward the deserving and punish the transgressors. The happy ending, which affirms the moral propriety of the universe, is a clear and definite characteristic of the fairy tale genre. Not only do Snow White, Cinderella, the soldier in "The Blue Light," and the young hero of "The Devil with the Three Golden Hairs" win their respective mates and hearts' desires (castles and kingdoms), their evil adversaries are consistently punished, either as the result of social justice (a court of law passing sentence on them) or as a result of cosmic justice (nature or the supernatural realm imposing some penalty, as, for example, when the birds peck out the stepsisters' eyes in "Cinderella").

A fourth quality of the fairy tale is that the audience is encouraged to identify strongly with the central protagonist, who is presented in an unambiguous way. The texts are solely focused on this individual, and he or she is represented as being a good and deserving, albeit modest and somewhat ordinary, person, who is being unfairly afflicted by a problem. The nicknames frequently used in fairy tales give some indication of the qualities of this typical protagonist—Cinderella or Aschenputtel, Simpleton or Thumbling, Hansel or Gretel, are ordinary and diminutive names denoting a person of not very impressive stature. Frequently, the protagonists have no name at all, but are referred to simply as "the boy" or "the girl." Generally, however, the outcome of the story serves to justify a reassessment of the protagonist, who turns out to be a princess or prince, or at least to be worthy of marrying a princess or prince.

One interesting issue raised by the characterization of the protagonists in these tales is that they frequently seem to be young people, engaged as a rule in the process of a finding a mate. Not all fairy tales are so focused; for example, "The Fisherman and His Wife" (AT 555) is about an old fisherman who lands a magic fish, but who, along with his wife, wastes his magic wishes. But there are sufficient examples to conclude tales are directed toward young people and appeal more to them than they do to adults. Furthermore, the central role of fantasy in this genre—it is used in a way that corroborates its existence rather than denying or rationalizing it away—would also seem to confirm a more childlike point of view, rather than the realistic and down-to-earth tone of other forms of folktales that are more popular with adults and that accordingly have predominantly adult protagonists. Thus the fairy tale functions to instruct the young about who they are, how they relate to others, and what they should know of the world.

In addition to the overtly recognizable characteristics of an unpretentious protagonist, the use of fantasy, an adventurous quest, and a happy ending, fairy tales may be said to be characterized by their thematic focus. Not only are the formal or stylistic features of these narratives distinctive, but their thematic subjects or focus may be seen as a delineating quality as well, as the following chapter will demonstrate.

2

The Thematic Core of Fairy Tales

Like fables, myths, legends, and other folk narratives, fairy tales are highly functional; that is, they address basic problems that confront their audiences. We can categorize these issues or fairy tale themes as falling into three major categories of human experience: the psychology of the individual, the sociology of the community, and the cosmology of the universe. In other words, fairy tales can be seen as telling us about our own feelings and psyches, as instructing us how to conform to society's expectations, and as offering spiritual guidance about how to see our place in the cosmos. In this chapter we will attempt to characterize the themes typifying fairy tales. In chapters 4 and 5 we will analyze how these themes are reflected in the narrative details of selected fairy tales.

Most of the psychological themes underlying fairy tales involve the concerns of young people, which is not surprising given the general orientation toward young protagonists of most fairy tales. The stories frequently depict the feelings or attitudes of the protagonists (with whom audiences are presumably identifying) toward parents, siblings, and prospective mates. The common psychological problems dramatized in fairy tales that concern the child's relationship to parents and other family members include feelings of rejection (separation anxiety), oppression (authoritarian or tyrannical anxieties), or jealousy (oedipal or sibling rivalry). In relation to prospective mates, the main issue dramatized appears to concern sexual anxieties.

In addition to offering psychological instruction, fairy tales frequently depict and inculcate social values. They promote marriage and the patriarchal family structure as dominant cultural institutions. They depict roles and behavior patterns considered socially appropriate for each gender and for each age group. They encourage industry and moral virtue (such as following the golden rule) as routes to securing material and financial success.

Finally, fairy tales offer guidance about the spiritual properties of the universe. They indicate the presence of supernatural powers or forces in the world that are reflections of a higher law. This law is characteristically Christian in European fairy tales, but it also frequently has a nondenominational or broadly mythic quality as well; that is, the spirits or powers are not always a part of orthodox Christian iconography, suggesting these tales may indeed predate Christianity. Furthermore, the cosmology depicted in fairy tale is also frequently connected to social institutions, suggesting that these institutions are "natural," that is, cosmically sanctioned and therefore justified.

The presence of these concerns in the stories may be regarded as a definitional characteristic of fairy tales inasmuch as part of the purpose of fairy tales appears to be to address these concerns through their symbolic depiction in the events of the story. In other words, fairy tales apparently serve a heuristic function, helping us to recognize and cope with typical problems and anxieties that we encounter in life. All of these issues may be regarded as of paramount interest to audience members who are trying to find their place in the world and answer life's enduring and perplexing questions. In particular, these issues seem to be of immediate and direct concern to young people who are still in the process of defining themselves, working through their feelings toward those with whom they are emotionally involved, establishing their place in society, learning and assimilating cultural norms, and determining their spiritual outlook.

For instance, one problem many children experience concerns their anxiety about being separated from their parents. This issue is frequently depicted in fairy tales by the protagonist's being abandoned or orphaned. For example, in "Three Hairs from the Devil's Beard" (AT 461), the protagonist is taken at birth and placed in a wooden chest, which is thrown in a river. In "Snow White" (AT 709), the heroine is expelled from her home. In "The Kind and Unkind Girls," the heroine falls down a well, or her stepmother compels her to jump in a well, to retrieve a shuttle that has fallen in.

Another common concern of childhood is the inclination to regard one or another of the parents as a tyrannical authority figure. The authoritarian problem is reflected in the preponderance of ogreish or witchlike parent figures who impose unreasonable demands upon the young protagonists. For example, in "The Maiden in the Tower" (AT 310) the mother figure locks the heroine up in her tower, while in "The Spirit in the Blue Light" (AT 562) the protagonist must chop an inordinate amount of wood for his dinner, and in "Three Hairs from the Devil's Beard," the king requires the protagonist to bring back three hairs from the devil's head or beard.

Generally, this authoritarian figure is of the same gender as the protagonist, which links this problem with the oedipal conflict. In other words, the oedipal rivalry is reflected in the predisposition of the protagonists of fairy tales to be in antagonistic opposition to older figures of the same sex. For example, in "The Boy Steals the Giant's Treasure" ("Jack and the Beanstalk"; AT 328) the protagonist is at odds with an ogreish giant who hoards his wealth (frequently gained at the youth's expense) and who wants to eat the protagonist. In one version of "Snow White," the heroine's mother breaks plates and glasses and demands that the husband choose between herself and her daughter. In "The Rabbit-Herd" (AT 570) the tyrannical king requires that the hero control the herd of wild rabbits or else suffer the loss of his life. The hero has his way with the king's wife as well as his daughter, before taking half of the king's lands. The oedipal rivalry is as much over gender roles—that is, competition for or anxiety about being recognized as a competent adult male or female, as fulfilling the role prescribed for men or women—as it is over the affection of the parent of the opposite sex (which, in the child's naive perspective, is coincidentally one of the qualifications of the gender role to which the child aspires).

Sibling rivalry is often reflected in fairy tales by the disadvantageous position of the protagonist relative to his or her siblings. For example, in "Cinderella" (AT 510) the heroine is generally made to sleep in the ashes while her sisters are treated like princesses. Similarly, in "The Kind and Unkind Girls" the heroine is mistreated in comparison to her stepsister, and the whole point is to reveal the heroine to be kind and deserving, the sister unkind and undeserving. And in "The Mouse (Cat, Frog, etc.) as Bride" (AT 402), although treated as insignificant by them, the hero outshines his siblings by bringing home the most beautiful ring, cloth, and bride.

These are just some of the typical concerns of children frequently depicted in the images, motifs, and events of fairy tales, as we will see in our discussion of some representative tales in subsequent chapters. Perhaps one of the most prevalent themes, and one curiously that seems to engender the most skepticism and resistance about its manifestation in fairy tales, concerns sexual maturation—the protagonist's relationship to the opposite sex and developing awareness of his or her own sexual identity. Perhaps because fairy tales are popularly believed to be for very young children, and these children are thought to be sexually innocent, or at least naive, the idea that many of these tales focus on sexual maturation seems unlikely and troubling to some people.

A major qualification needs to be made here, however, concerning the appearance of this theme in fairy tales, which might alleviate some of the difficulties in acknowledging it. We can divide fairy tales into at least three subcategories: tales for young children; tales for developing adolescents; and tales for relatively mature adults.[1] These subdivisions are made on the basis of the age of the protagonist, the nature of the problem tackled and the quest undertaken, and the form of resolution achieved.

In the tales for young children, by which we mean prepubescent children, the protagonists are obviously quite young, the problem concerns adjusting to family life at home, and the quest concerns acquiring or demonstrating the social and domestic skills needed to be accepted as a competent member of that family. The form of resolution achieved in these tales inevitably involves a successful return to the child's parental home, as for example in "The Kind and Unkind Girls" and "Hansel and Gretel" (AT 327A).

We might look more closely at "Hansel and Gretel" as an example of a fairy tale for young children. The protagonists are so young they do not even realize that the bread crumbs will be eaten by the birds. The problem they face is that there is not enough food at home to feed the entire family. The lack of food may be read as a metaphor for there not being enough love at home. In essence, the children feel unloved and unwanted, as reflected in the stepmother's desire to abandon them. In their quest they must demonstrate their competence in dealing with life's problems, such as finding one's way back home, avoiding the evil clutches of a wicked and voracious witch, and crossing a river, in order to reaffirm their rightful place in the family. The little boy ultimately proves too immature to handle the first problem successfully, so the heroine must take matters into her own hands and deceive the wicked witch, manage the river crossing, and restore the happy home. The fact that the children return home after solving the problem reveals that this is a tale directed at prepubescent children, whose world is still exclusively the world of their parents.

We can see, furthermore, that this tale illustrates the confrontation of an oedipal conflict by the young protagonist. The fact that it is the heroine who ultimately demonstrates her competence makes her the protagonist, and the fact that the destruction of the evil witch coincides with the disappearance of the unpleasant mother figure who instigated the expulsion of the children suggests that this tale illustrates an oedipal conflict between the young girl and her mother. The evil witch would be an exaggerated representation of the unpleasant aspects of the mother, at least from the young girl's point of view. The correlation between the concern for food on the mother's part and the excessive appetite of the witch is no accident—it is a symbolic connection between the two characters. By eliminating the witchlike aspect of the mother, the young heroine may be seen as overcoming her fear of and resentment toward a mother figure. Thus, we see that one subgenre of the fairy tale includes tales about prepubescent protagonists who confront problems afflicting young people still living at home, such as getting along with, overcoming one's hostility toward, or defeating the perceived oppression by a family member.

In the tales for developing adolescents, which is the largest subdivision of the fairy tale genre, the protagonists are postpubescent adolescents who are in the process of leaving their parents' home and finding one of their own, and the problems they face generally concern the difficulties of acquiring a mate. The quest accordingly involves finding the mate and overcoming the obstacles to marriage, and the resolution of the quest entails the establishing of a new domicile as a residence for the newly married couple.

As an example of this group of fairy tales, we might consider "Dick Wittington's Cat" (known as "The Cat as Helper"; AT 545). In this tale the protagonist is a young man. His father dies, which signals the protagonist's need to move out of his dependent role in his parents' household and establish his own autonomous life. He no longer can rely upon or look up to a dominant and protective father figure; it is now time to be on his own. An element of sibling rivalry is reflected in the competition with his brothers, who inherit the bulk of the father's estate. All the protagonist gets is the care of an old cat, which he willingly undertakes in order to keep the cat from starving. The protagonist in this act not only reveals his moral propriety and compassion (his willingness to watch out for his fellow creatures), but also evidences his developing maturity—his readiness and ability to care for something else, or someone else, which is a major step toward adulthood.

The young man now needs to acquire a kingdom, which is symbolic of economic security, and a mate. The cat, out of gratitude, offers to help. The problem is that the young man apparently has no skill or wealth. The quest is to demonstrate his worth and win his kingdom, and the cat is instrumental in fulfilling these goals, which shows that the young man received something of value from his father after all, even if it seemed insignificant at the time. The story suggests that the nonmaterialistic legacy of the parents is more valuable and important than the money and goods they may give to their offspring. The magical assistance of the cat not only confirms the propriety of the young man's morality, but also demonstrates the efficacy of that moral principle in the universe; that supernatural powers come to his aid is a confirmation of both the potency and the validity of his moral beliefs. The cat manages to fool a king into thinking the young man is enormously wealthy by pretending that the lands, cattle, and castle of an ogre are the protagonist's. It is a brave bluff, validating the young man's courage as well as his ingenuity, and he is rewarded for his ambition by receiving the king's daughter for a wife.

The pretense reveals furthermore a certain philosophical assessment, that ownership is essentially superficial and illusory, a social charade that we play among ourselves. By playing this charade better than the king, the young man profits both materially (he is given half the kingdom as a dowry) and emotionally (he is given the king's daughter in marriage). Once again, the means of acquiring the benefits of material success serve to illustrate their essential subordination to higher principles and laws in the cosmos. The conclusion of the tale reveals that the focus of the story is on the young person's path to adulthood, particularly the part concerning leaving home, establishing a domain of one's own, and finding a mate. These are the concerns of the developing adolescent.

In the third and final category of fairy tales, the protagonists are mature adults, already married, and their problems seem to concern reconciling themselves to the vicissitudes and difficulties of daily life, particularly the emotional travails of living with a mate. The problems in these tales concern moral and philosophical dilemmas, such as fidelity in a marriage, communication between partners, or adjusting to the birth of children. The quests undertaken lead to the reconciliation of the husband and wife, their acceptance of each other and themselves, and the restoration of domestic tranquility.

An example of this group of tales is "The Three Golden Sons" (AT 707), which is one of a whole cycle of tales concerning a calumniated wife. The protagonist is an adult married woman who is about to give birth when her husband is called away. The problem surfaces when an antagonistic figure, sometimes a sibling or a parent figure, acts as a midwife and steals the child away after the delivery and either substitutes a dog or some other animal for the child, or else just smears blood on the mother's mouth and accuses her of eating her child. Alternatively, the protagonist's letter to her husband is intercepted and is changed to read that she gave birth to an animal. His response that she should be cared for until he returns is also changed to read that she should be expelled. The protagonist is accordingly cast out of her husband's home and must seek shelter elsewhere.

One main problem depicted in this tale is anxiety about childbirth. The protagonist is evidently anxious about the consequences of becoming a mother. The image of giving birth to animals suggests a fear about what will be born as well as a possible concern that childbirth is somehow an inherently animalistic activity. Furthermore, the idea of being accused of eating one's children, or otherwise injuring or losing them through lack of attention, may be an expression of latent fears in the young mother about her own competence or about attitudes toward her as a competent mother. Finally, some concern about the husband's response to childbirth and about the effect of childbirth on his relationship to the heroine is apparently manifested in the motif of the altered letters, in which a hostile reaction to the birth of a child is fictionally presented and results in the rejection of the heroine by her husband.

The quest undertaken by the heroine is to find a new home and rebuild her life. In some versions of the tales that depict this calumniation of the heroine, she is taken in by fairies who magically care for her. The husband returns, undertakes an extensive search for her, and comes as a supplicant to her residence. This conclusion reaffirms for the heroine that her husband still loves her and that there is a solid foundation in their relationship, which will not be altered by the birth of a child. It also suggests the importance of the protagonist's achieving some autonomy in the relationship, as reflected in the successful establishment of a place of residence of her own. The resolution of the problem also suggests that the heroine can rely on hidden or nonrational aspects of herself or of the cosmos to aid her in this quest, inasmuch as the fairies come to her assistance.

In other versions of this tale type, the heroine's children effect her reconciliation by setting out to find their father. Through the magic objects they achieve, they win the attention of the king, who then discovers who they are and restores them and their mother to their rightful place. The emphasis in this account is on the redemptive potential in the children, the hope that they will ultimately confirm for the husband, as well as for the paternalistic society, the heroine's true worth. Thus, these fairy tales for adults address certain anxieties and problems that may typically afflict audience members as they face the challenges of marriage and parenthood. Once again, these anxieties and problems are presented in exaggerated and fantastic motifs that symbolically suggest the underlying concerns motivating the narrative.

In sum, there are three different kinds of fairy tales for different audiences. It is only logical that each kind tends to focus on concerns typifying its particular audience group. It should not be surprising to find that tales with young children as protagonists tend to focus on issues about relating to parents and on achieving recognition of social competence, that tales with adolescent protagonists mostly concern themselves with sexual maturation and finding a mate, and that tales with adult protagonists generally treat marital stress and other difficulties of adult daily life. These issues are of primary concern to the respective age groups. The tales were created by storytellers as entertainment for their audiences, and what audiences find most entertaining and riveting is to see their own lives and concerns fictionally dramatized for them. We should note, furthermore, that in the other genres of the folktale, the same age-specific subcategories manifest themselves, for example, children's jokes versus adolescent jokes versus adult jokes. Fairy tales are thus one genre or class of folktales that appeal to audiences of different age groups and that may be subdivided by their focus on one or another of these audiences.

We can classify or subdivide fairy tales based on our identification of other specific audiences as well. For instance, we can differentiate tales that appeal to female versus male audience members. The concerns for each gender (both generally and within each of the age groups identified above) are somewhat different, as are the social mores and expectations for each gender. Some scholars (such as Sandra Gilbert, Jack Zipes, Ruth Bottigheimer) have pointed out that this gender-based distinction reveals a sexist bias in many versions of fairy tales, and perhaps even in the inherent structure of the tales themselves.[2] For example, the protagonist of female fairy tales are said to be encouraged to be passive and wait to be rescued from their problems, while the protagonists of male fairy tales are said to be encouraged to be active and to undertake the resolution of their problems on their own initiative and to redress the inequities or moral transgressions themselves. In chapters 4 and 5, fairy tales with male and female protagonists will be analyzed to identify not just the issue of gender difference, but also of gender bias.

Another basis for subcategorizing fairy tales would be cultural. That is, the fairy tales, or versions of fairy tales, that are popular in one ethnic community or nation may be differentiated from those popular in another community or nation. These distinctions are reflected not only in the language and stylistic preferences, but also in the selection of motifs used to tell the stories as well as the social customs and cultural perspectives reflected. Indeed, some scholars are uncomfortable with analysis of fairy tales or versions of fairy tales apart from this cultural context. There is no question that each version of a fairy tale is indelibly marked by its cultural context. Storytellers are not completely autonomous and insulated individuals; they are the product of the communities and cultures in which they live. Similarly, audiences generally have a cultural orientation that also contributes not only to what stories are asked for and enjoyed, but also to the way they are told. One further argument for the cultural classification of fairy tales (that is, of studying French fairy tales apart from German ones) is that these ethnic and cultural divisions tend to cut across age boundaries; in other words, the same cultural values and attitudes that we might find in French children's fairy tales, or versions of fairy tales, would also be found in French fairy tales told for adolescents or adults. Thus, the cultural divisions would seem on one level to transcend or supersede the age-group classification.

One limitation to classifying fairy tales according to ethnic or cultural boudaries, however, is that a relatively small percentage (certainly less than half) of the fairy tales circulating in a given cultural group are distinctive or unique to that community. In contrast, the tales with age-specific protagonists, are almost exclusively told with protagonists of that age. It is extremely rare to find a version of "Cinderella" or "The Kind and Unkind Girls" featuring an adult protagonist (although there are some exceptions), whereas there are numerous versions from different cultures. Furthermore, since the ethnically specific elements of these tales do not appear outside the particular esoteric community, they have secondary importance for those studying the larger phenomenon of the genre. Mostly what we find in the collections from various communities are distinctive versions, not original tales. As the Italian proverb puts it: the fairy tale has no landlord. It does not reside in or belong to a single place, person, or culture. Thus, the specific ethnic or cultural values that we find in fairy tales seem to be for the most part superimposed upon the tales or on the basic structure of the tales. This structure and the core of themes that could be said to generate it apparently transcend the cultural renditions of it.

What we are confronted with is a broadly cross-cultural phenomenon, with hundreds of versions of tales that are popular from China to Europe, as well as on the African and American continents. In trying to account for this culturally widespread expressive phenomenon, we might be inclined to go as far as Carl Jung and Joseph Campbell and hypothesize that it indicates a universal appeal to the human spirit, that the genre inherently addresses fundamental questions of human existence that appeal to all races, and that, accordingly, the key to the meaning and popularity of fairy tales may be found by looking on this universal level. But not all fairy tales do appeal to all cultural groups; while the various cultural communities on the European continent share a large number of basic tale types, the same cannot be said for African, Native American, Asian, or Oceanic peoples. While most of the communities in these regions have tales that could be generally considered fairy tales, in that they have ordinary protagonists who encounter magic on their quests, in tone and in other regards, these tales are recognizably different from the class of tales from European tradition that we have come to call fairy tales.

Thus, geographical proximity and diffusion obviously play a role in the spread of fairy tales and in the form they assume in various regions of the world. Although the tale types do cross certain specific or local cultural boundaries, the fact that they are less capable of crossing major cultural boundaries, such as those between Asian or African and European cultural groups, would suggest that there are certain basic cultural assumptions that color these narratives in some essential way. Accordingly, we cannot simplistically conclude that these are pan-humanistic tales; although they do seem to address certain fundamental concerns that are of interest to all people, the form they take is marked to some extent by their cultural ancestry. In studying fairy tales we must balance an understanding of their fundamental philosophical themes that cross cultural boundaries with an appreciation of their basic ethnic or social values and characteristics that mark their specific cultural affiliation.

In sum, the fairy tale in oral tradition is a very complex phenomenon. It appeals to different groups and different ages, sometimes for the same reasons and sometimes for different reasons. The most we can conclude is that the fairy tale is a narrative genre with numerous examples that manifest in common the basic characteristics that we have already identified:

- the incorporation of magic or fantasy in such a manner that its epistemological and ontological validity is affirmed;
- the incorporation of a quest, adventure, or problem, which entails interaction with the unknown or magical realm;
- the successful completion of that quest or problem, in such a manner that the moral propriety of the universe is affirmed;
- the incorporation of an ordinary protagonist with whom we are to identify unambiguously and who is typically a young person;
- the depiction of themes of basic interest to age-differentiated audiences about typical concerns of their lives.

In this relatively short study, we cannot begin to document comprehensively the extent of the conformance of most tales that fall within this genre to these characteristics (nor even to review the vast scholarly basis for these conclusions). There are simply too many such narratives. Summarizing the plots alone would take more than 100 pages, as demonstrated in chapter 2 of Thompson's *The Folktale,* where this task has already, for the most part, been completed. I must simply refer readers to *The Folktale* and to the companion text, *The Types of the Folktale,* in order to assess the applicability of this generic definition to a comprehensive compilation of fairy tale examples. Instead of a broad survey, in chapters 4 and 5 I will provide an in-depth examination of the way that selected fairy tales exemplify the essential properties of this genre as they have been outlined in this chapter and the preceding one—first by analyzing some fairy tales with male protagonists and then comparatively discussing some with female protagonists. Before we can undertake this analysis of these selected fairy tales, however, we should first consider the evolution of the folk fairy tale in written literature. The fairy tale genre has had a significant impact on written literature, as the next chapter will demonstrate.

3

The Literary History of the Fairy Tale

Having acknowledged that the fairy tale genre is initially the product of folklore, we should note that, for most literate peoples, the oral tradition itself is not the main source for their exposure to the genre of fairy tales. Because of the diminished popularity of the fairy tale genre in the oral culture of literate societies (replaced by jokes and personal experience narratives to a large extent), editions of collected fairy tales, such as the Grimms' anthology, have become our primary resource for these stories. The situations for oral storytelling that led traditionally to the performance of versions of fairy tales in the past, such as long winter evenings without radio or television for entertainment, are not as common in modern literate societies, and, as a result, the longer and more sophisticated narrative genre of the fairy tale is not widely practiced by the folk (which is to say us). Our oral traditions now serve other purposes, and we have come to rely upon redacted texts to provide versions of the classic fairy tales that entertained so many previous generations. There are literally thousands of these collections of fairy tales, from all over the world, and they make available a wonderfully rich heritage of storytelling. We shall endeavor later in this chapter to provide a brief literary history of some of the most important collections.

However, we should recognize first that these edited collections of oral versions are to some extent hybrids of folklore and literature. They replicate the oral texts reasonably faithfully in many cases, but they nonetheless inevitably alter the oral experience to some extent, and, in some cases, even seriously tamper with those "texts."[1] For example, the stylistic modifications introduced by Wilhelm Grimm into the Grimm collection have been extensively discussed by various scholars (Linda Dégh, Maria Tatar, Bottigheimer).[2] Thus, these fairy tale collections represent a distinctive form of the fairy tale, different from that of oral tradition. They are a valuable and entertaining source for developing our awareness of the broad tradition of fairy tales, but they should not be regarded as being exactly equivalent to the oral tradition, even when they are performed by single narrators.

Another important form of the fairy tale is that produced by literary authors, such as Hans Christian Andersen, Washington Irving, John Ruskin, Charles Dickens, Oscar Wilde, and Carlo Collodi in the nineteenth century, and L. Frank Baum, Edith Nesbit, Howard Pyle, Antoine de Saint-Exupéry, P. L. Travers, Mary Norton, E. B. White, T. H. White, Ursula K. Le Guin, J. R. R. Tolkien, Madeleine L'Engle, and Maurice Sendak in the twentieth, who have used the fairy tale model to create original stories that imitate the oral genre.[3] These authors employ in their narratives the generic characteristics of an ordinary hero or heroine who is engaged on a quest and who encounters marvelous or fantastic phenomena or events that are to be taken seriously, and who ultimately triumphs in his or her quest. We must distinguish here, however, between these literary texts that treat as serious and epistemologically valid the fantastic element of the fairy tale genre that they present and those literary treatments that employ the fantastic element explicitly for satiric or didactic uses. For example, Jonathan Swift's *Gulliver's Travels* does not qualify as a fairy tale, since the fantasy in this case is used for satiric purposes and is not presented as a valid representation of the world.[4]

Similarly, we must distinguish literary fairy tales from literary versions of another related genre, animal fables. In animal fables, the only violation of the empirical perception of reality is that the animal characters talk and act like humans. If we regard this personification as a literary device, the tales then work rather straightforwardly as narrative illustrations of realistic human conditions and behavior, as in, for example, Aesop's fables or the fables of Reynard the Fox.[5] Fables do not necessarily evoke, as fairy tales do, a sense of the wonder, of the magical properties, in the universe. Thus, literary animal fables like Kenneth Grahame's *The Wind in the Willows* (1908), George Orwell's *Animal Farm* (1946), and Richard Adams' *Watership Down* (1972) do not fall under the rubric of fairy tales.[6] Similarly, certain animal stories are related to and function more like myths, in that they offer explanatory accounts of how the world is shaped. Thus, literary versions of these animal myths, such as Rudyard Kipling's *Just So Stories* (1902), Thornton W. Burgess's *Mother West Wind "How" Stories* (1927), or "The Piper at the Gates of Dawn" chapter in *The Wind in the Willows*, would not be classified as fairy tales.[7] Separating out the satires, animal fables, and myths of literature, we are still left with a large and impressive assortment of literary texts that emulate the fairy tale model.

So, our conception of the fairy tale genre recognizes three major forms: indigenous oral versions, collected and variously edited versions in print, and original, single-author fairy tales that are not drawn from oral tradition but that closely resemble that narrative genre. Inasmuch as we surveyed the form and nature of the oral fairy tales in chapter 1, in this chapter we will attempt to survey some major examples of the other two forms of the fairy tale genre—edited collections and literary imitations.

Working from Stith Thompson's *The Folktale* (which has already surveyed the classic collections of fairy tales), we find that perhaps the oldest literary collection that includes some fairy tales comes to us from Indian tradition, specifically in the collection entitled the *Panchatantra*.[8] For example, the *Panchatantra* includes a version of "The Magician and His Pupil" (AT 325; Thompson, 69). A father apprentices his son to a magician in order to learn his art, but part of the bargain is that the father must recognize the boy at the end of a year. The hero learns the magic secretly and then must flee when his master discovers his abilities. The son then has his father sell him in a magically disguised form (as a horse or an ox) to various buyers from whom he then escapes. Finally, the father inadvertently sells his son as a horse to the magician, and he mistakenly includes the bridle that keeps the son enchanted. The son manages to strip off the bridle and conquer the magician in a battle of magical transformations. Frequently, the hero tricks the magician into becoming a cock whose head he then bites off when the hero assumes the form of a fox.

The *Panchatantra* also includes a version of "Luck and Intelligence" (AT 945), in which a peasant, in order to win a princess from her father by breaking her silence, tells her a story about a wood-carver who carves a doll, a tailor who dresses her, and a gardener (himself) who gives her the power of speech (Thompson, 143). He then asks her to whom the doll belongs, and she replies; however, when the king refuses to fulfill his bargain, the peasant must rely on luck rather than on intelligence to extricate himself from the king's sentence of death. In addition there occurs in the *Panchatantra* a contest between an ogre and a hero in which the hero tricks the ogre into believing he can squeeze milk from a stone, while in reality he is really squeezing cheese, much like the central episode in many versions of "The Brave Tailor" (AT 1640; Thompson, 144).

This fairy tale motif of tricking an ogre or giant occurs as well in another collection from India, *The Ocean of Story* from the eleventh century (Thompson, 76).[9] This motif is part of the tale entitled "Devils (Giants) Fight over Magic Objects" (AT 518), in which the hero tells three devils he will help them decide who should get the magic hat that renders the wearer invisible. When they give it to him, he disappears. This tricky acquisition of a magic object occurs widely in many of the classic fairy tale collections, such as the *The Arabian Nights Entertainments, or The Thousand and One Nights* (Thompson, 76).[10] Also in *The Ocean of Story* is a version of "Faithful John" (AT 516), in which a servant is falsely accused of treachery toward his master since he acts upon knowledge that has been magically acquired and cannot be related upon penalty of petrification (Thompson, 112). He ultimately tells the master the reason for his actions just before he is about to be executed, and after he has been turned to stone, the master makes a great sacrifice to restore the servant to life.

There are a number of tales that appear not only in *The Ocean of Story* but also in the classic collection of fairy tales from the

Middle East, the *Thousand and One Nights*. For example, we find in both collections versions of "The Prince's Wings" (AT 575), where a prince makes use of some magical wings to make off with a princess and returns only when her father offers half the kingdom as a reward (Thompson, 78). Similarly, "The Girl as Helper in the Hero's Flight" (AT 313), with its introductory episode of the swan maidens, occurs in both collections (Thompson, 88). In this tale a hero sees the heroine transform herself into a swan and pursues her. He marries her and then loses her when she finds her wings again one day, and then he must undertake a long journey to recover her. Alternatively, he completes various difficult tasks to win her from her father or the ogre who guards her, and then must flee with her. (This is essentially the plot of the legend of Jason and Medea and the story of "Culwich and Olwen" in *The Mabinogion*.[11] Ultimately, the hero rescues the heroine from an ogre's power, frequently by means of a magic flight.

The *Thousand and One Nights* is our source for a great many fairy tales, such as "Open Sesame" (AT 676), in which the young hero learns the secret password for a robbers' treasure den and makes use of the gold to outwit his brother (Thompson, 68). Perhaps the most well-known tale from the *Thousand and One Nights* is "Aladdin and His Wonderful Lamp" (AT 561), in which the hero acquires a magic lamp, which he uses to obtain a princess and a kingdom (Thompson, 71). Another well-known tale, one that is closely related to "Aladdin's Lamp" in its basic plot motivation, is "The Spirit in the Bottle" (AT 331), in which a man inadvertently releases a genie who has been imprisoned for many years (Thompson, 47). Rather than reward the man, the genie intends to kill him out of his anger for being imprisoned so long. The man manages to fool the genie into returning to the bottle and then lets him out again only when the genie swears to do his bidding. A less well-known but no less popular fairy tale is "The Two Travelers" (AT 613), which is found in the *Thousand and One Nights* as well as in Basile's *Pentamerone* (Thompson, 80). In this tale, after a man is blinded by his traveling companion, he settles under a tree and (like the servant in "Faithful John") overhears birds or spirits talking. He uses the magically acquired wisdom to restore his sight, cure a princess, and perform other miraculous deeds for which he is richly rewarded.

Another well-known tale from the *Thousand and One Nights* is "The Tsar's Dog (Sidi Numan)" (AT 449), which is closely related to "The Faithless Wife" (AT 315B, Thompson, 115). In both tales the wife is unfaithful and endeavors to eliminate her husband in favor of a rival; in the former she magically turns the hero into a dog, while in the latter, he transforms himself into various animals to escape his wife's murderous attempts on his life (much as in "The Magician and His Pupil"). The *Thousand and One Nights* also has one of the earliest versions of "The Bird, The Horse, and the Princess" (AT 550), which has reappeared in many literary versions since (Thompson, 107). A king orders a quest for a bird that has been stealing golden apples from his orchard (or for some other similarly magical object). The youngest brother of three succeeds in the quest where his brothers failed because of his kindness and courtesy. His brothers rob and imprison him, but he manages to survive and claim the king's daughter as his bride. Another very popular tale in the *Thousand and One Nights* that has been retold in literary collections over the years is "The Animal Languages" (AT 670; Thompson, 83). In it a man learns the language of animals after rescuing a snake, but he may tell no one about his gift upon pain of death. When his wife badgers him into agreeing to relate his secret, he makes preparations for his death, but before he can tell her, he overhears his barnyard animals criticizing him for not being able to maintain discipline in the house comparable to the discipline enforced in the barnyard. He decides not to tell his wife.

The *Thousand and One Nights* also includes a version of another very popular narrative about a slandered wife who is accused of killing or eating her children or of giving birth to animals (Thompson, 120–5). This tale employs a motif frequently found in various tale types: a woman is calumniated as a result of someone's substituting false letters for those sent between the woman and her husband. The wife is expelled as a result of the false letters. This sequence of events forms the core of a number of related tale types, which introduce some variations in the introduction and conclusion of the story. These tale types include "Born from a Fish" (AT 705), "The Maiden Without Hands" (AT 706), "The Three Golden Sons" (AT 707), and "Crescentia" (AT 712). In addition to its appearance in the *Thousand and One Nights*, there have been numerous literary retellings of this basic narrative, for example, Chaucer's "The Man of Law's Tale" (Thompson, 121).[12] The *Thousand and One Nights* also contains a repository of a version of the widely recognized narrative of "Polyphemus" (AT 1137), in which the hero escapes from a murderous giant ogre by blinding him with a burning log (Thompson, 200).

We can see that the *Thousand and One Nights* is a major repository of fairy tale plots. However, we should note that, as in the *Panchatantra*, these plots have been reworked in a decidedly literary fashion, such that the style of the narrative and sometimes even the elements and motifs employed to relate the plots are far removed from folk tradition and resemble more the third form of fairy tales, literary creations. Similarly, Boccaccio's *Decameron*, Straparola's *Pleasant Nights*, and Basile's *Pentamerone*, which are equally important anthologies of fairy tale plots from the Italian fourteenth, sixteenth, and seventeenth centuries respectively, retell many traditional fairy tale plots but incorporate considerable stylistic modifications.[13] As Stith Thompson notes, "These prose tale collections, beginning as early as Boccaccio's *Decameron*, sometimes contain stories which the author had heard, though they are usually much changed in style from what must have been the oral original. Such is true of 'The Smith Outwits the Devil' (Type 330), and of 'Six Go Through the Whole World' (Type 513)" (Thompson, 182). Thompson goes on to identify the fairy tale plots found in Straparola's and Basile's collections:

> In the *Pleasant Nights* of Straparola in the sixteenth century are versions of: The Magician and His Pupil (Type 325); The Youth who Wanted to Learn What Fear Is (Type 326); The Youth Transformed to a Horse (Type 314); Cap o'Rushes (Type 510B); The Three Golden Sons (Type 707); Our Lady's Child (Type 710); The Cat Castle (Type 545A); Puss in Boots (Type 545B); and The Lazy Boy (Type 675).
>
> An even longer list of oral tales is found for the first time in the *Pentamerone* of Basile, 1634–1636. Among them are: The Maiden in the Tower (Type 310); The Black and White Bride (Type 403); The Three Oranges (Type 408); Little Brother and Little Sister (Type 450); The Maiden Who Seeks Her Brothers (Type 451); The Spinning-Woman by the Spring (Type 480); The Three Old Women Helpers (Type 501); Dungbeetle (Type 559); The Magic Ring (Type 560); The Louse-Skin (Type 621); The Carnation (Type 652); Snow-White (Type 709). (Thompson 182)

Charles Perrault's collection of eight fairy tales, *Contes du Ma Mère L'Oye Tales of Mother Goose)*, published in France in 1697, is perhaps the most important collection of fairy tales to appear after the Italian collections and prior to the great folktale collections of the nineteenth century.[14] While it contains only eight tales, the appeal of the individual tales and the enormous popularity of this collection as a whole make it a significant source for familiarity with the fairy tale genre. His version of "Cinderella" is particularly well-known and is credited by some scholars for having been responsible for disseminating the motif of the glass slipper, since according to these scholars the slipper was more commonly made of fur before Perrault's collection appeared. Similarly, his version of "Sleeping Beauty" (AT 410) has been very influential and is apparently the source, to some extent, for the version of that tale that the Grimms published (see Jones, "In Defense of the Grimms"). Perrault also included a French version of "The Kind and Unkind Girls." We should note that Perrault was a member of the French Academy, and he took great liberties—or great pains, depending on one's point of view—in rewriting the style of the folk fairy tales that he or his son had collected. Perrault's style is florid, his tone self-conscious and didactic. His ending for "Little Red Riding Hood," for example, is quite moralistic, presenting a warning for young girls who stray from the beaten path. Perrault influenced various French writers of the time, as seen for example in the literary imitations of fairy tales produced by Madame d'Aulnoy (e.g., "The Cat as Helper," AT 545, and "The Three Golden Sons," AT 707) and Madame de Beaumont (e.g., "Beauty and the Beast," AT 425C).[15]

Perhaps the most significant collection in the eighteenth century was J. K. Musäus's *Volksmärchen der Deutschen (Folktales of Germany)*, in part because it anticipated the Grimms' collection.[16] Among other fairy tales, Musäus retold a version of "Snow White." Once again, however, the folk tradition is not closely adhered to, and Musäus substantially alters the tale's elements, such as introducing historical figures to play the leading roles.

With the Grimms' collection, published as *Kinder- und Hausmärchen* between 1812 and 1815, came perhaps one of the first attempts (at least in the first edition) to provide not only a reasonably comprehensive collection of the stories of the folk, but also a sense of the authentic style and language in which they were told. Ironically, while these qualities of the Grimms' initial edition make this a landmark collection of fairy tales for folklorists and thus would seem to have been the logical basis for its historical significance, it was Wilhelm Grimms' subsequent literary editing (revising the style and publishing an abbreviated collection of only 50 of the most popular tales) that eventually made that collection the best-selling one in Germany and assured its preeminent place in the subsequent literary history of fairy tales.

As Maria Tatar suggests, the idea for the abbreviated collection came from the publication in England in 1823 of a similarly abbreviated selection translated by Edgar Taylor, which sold very well and whose financial success Wilhelm wished to duplicate in Germany (Tatar, 19–20). The first edition had been criticized as having a slovenly style and as being too long and expensive, so the revised and abbreviated edition was much preferred. The scholarship on the Grimms' collection and the various editions it went through (seven) is extensive; readers might wish to consult studies by Tatar, Bottigheim, and Heinz Rölleke for further discussion of this major collection of fairy tales.[17] Of particular interest are arguments about the sexism and Christian moralizing Wilhelm is said to have introduced to the texts. Bottigheimer notes, for example, that Wilhelm took dialogue away from the good female characters and gave it to men or to evil female characters, perhaps to illustrate his personal (and society's) view that silence in women was a virtue (Bottigheimer, "Silenced Women," 115–31). This deactivating of the good female characters certainly results in a biased depiction of women in the collection.

From the perspective of literary history, the popularity of the Grimms' *Kinder- und Hausmärchen* served as a catalyst to writers and especially collectors in Europe, such that in the nineteenth century there occurred a veritable explosion of similar collections. Some of the most noteworthy include those by Andrew Lang, *The Blue Fairy Book* (1889) and a series of successors of various colors (red, yellow, green, etc.); Edwin Hartland, *English Fairy and Folk Tales* (1890); Joseph Jacobs, *English Fairy Tales* (1890), *Celtic Fairy Tales* (1892); W. B. Yeats, *Fairy and Folk Tales of Ireland* (1892); Peter Christen Asbjörsen and Jörgen Moe, *Norwegian Folktales* (also published as *East of the Sun, West of the Moon* and translated in 1859 by George Dascent in *Popular Tales from the Norse)*; Hans Christian Andersen, *Fairytales* (first published in Denmark in 1835, translated in 1846); Emmanuel Cosquin, *Contes Populaires de Lorraine* (1887); and A. N. Afanasief, *Russian Folktales* (translated in 1873). These collections served the same seminal function for their respective language groups that the Grimms' did for German-speaking people: they introduced the literate audience to the wealth of folk fairy tales circulating among their own people, many of which were versions of tales found in other cultures as well.

Part of the motivation for these collections was the developing nationalism of the early and middle nineteenth century, but ironically, as a consequence of the proliferation of collections from various countries, the international existence, and indeed the international citizenship, of many of the narratives came to light. No longer could various cultural groups think of owning or having exclusive dominion over selected tales, as more and more versions of these tales were collected from around the world. They led inevitably to the comprehensive index of tale types first produced by Antti Aarne and later expanded by Stith Thompson. Ultimately, these numerous collections, in documenting for the literate audience the wealth of narrative material that circulated in oral tradition, confirmed the extraordinary breadth of the fairy tale as a major art form. The ingenuity, imagination, and artistry of oral narration began finally to become recognized by cultures that had been under the spell of literacy for centuries.

Not only did the proliferation of fairy tale collections establish concretely the importance of the folk fairy tale as a major literary genre, it also extended its traditional influence on budding writers. More and more examples of literary imitations of the fairy tale began to appear in the nineteenth century. For example, in England we find fairy tales being written by Charles Dickens *(The Magic Fishbone* and *A Christmas Carol)*, John Ruskin *(The King of the Golden River)*, Oscar Wilde *(The Happy Prince and Other Fairy Stories)*, William Makepeace Thackeray *(The Rose and the Ring)*, Robert Southey *(The Story of the Three Bears)*, Charles Kingsley *(The Water Babies)*, Howard Pyle *(Pepper and Salt)*, George MacDonald *(At the Back of the North Wind)*, and many others.

In America, Washington Irving's sojourn in Germany led to his writing "Rip Van Winkle" and "The Legend of Sleepy

Hollow" in *The Sketch Book of Geoffrey Crayon, Gent.* Nathaniel Hawthorne retold myths, legends, and some fairy tales in his collections of *Tanglewood Tales for Boys and Girls* and *A Wonder Book for Boys and Girls,* and a fairy tale influence may be discerned in many of his other texts, such as *The Marble Faun* and "Feathertop." John Greenleaf Whittier produced a collection entitled *The Supernaturalism of New England,* which included some fairy tales. Edgar Allen Poe incorporated fairy tale elements in "The Fall of the House of Usher" and "Eleanora," although it should be noted that while his protagonists go on quests and encounter fantastic phenomena, they do not succeed in their quests as a rule, and the moral propriety of the universe is by no means upheld.[18] Similarly, Melville's *The Confidence Man* has the element of fantasy and shape-shifting borrowed from fairy tales, but it is without the uplifting moral vision.[19] Even Mark Twain, the consummate realist, borrows the fairy tale adventure plot for *Tom Sawyer* and *Huckleberry Finn* and dabbles freely in the fantasy of fairy tales in his *A Connecticut Yankee in King Arthur's Court* by having his protagonist magically journey across time and geography.[20]

At the start of the twentieth century, we find some major literary successes borrowing the fairy tale formula. Helen Bannerman's *Little Black Sambo* offers a literary reworking of the narratives typical of the prepubescent subgenre of fairy tales—a young boy encounters a threat to his life but manages to outwit it and return home to a meal of pancakes. Similarly, L. Frank Baum's *The Wizard of Oz* and James Barrie's *Peter Pan,* both of which appeared at the turn of the century and were very well received, are prepubescent fantasies that draw heavily on fairy tale elements, specifically the confrontation of supernatural adversaries and magical phenomena by young protagonists who manage to overcome their fears and foes and return safely and happily home. Twenty years later, Hugh Lofting employed the popular fairy tale motif of speaking animals in *The Story of Dr. Dolittle* and various sequels. At mid-century C. S. Lewis's *The Lion, the Witch, and the Wardrobe,* J. R. R. Tolkien's *The Hobbit* and *The Lord of the Rings,* Mary Norton's *The Borrowers,* and E. B. White's *Charlotte's Web* and *Stuart Little* were published and achieved considerable acclaim. They each depicted a protagonist's exploration of magical worlds and the spiritual and personal enlightenment that accrues from the enlarged sense of the world promoted by these explorations. Later in the century Dr. Seuss had his child protagonists encounter magical cats and other creatures (for example, in *The Cat in the Hat*), while Maurice Sendak's *Where the Wild Things Are* had his young hero confront his own wild side in a journey to the magical realm of the wild things.

These are simply some of the high-water marks of the fairy tale's influence on English literature. For reasons of economy, they are chosen exclusively from the English language tradition. Carlo Collodi's *The Adventures of Pinocchio*, Antoine du Saint-Exupéery's *The Little Prince,* and many of Hans Christen Andersen's original tales are just a few of the many non-English literary texts that incorporate fairy tales and that could be added to the list of important literary emulations of the fairy tale. Readers should consult Jack Zipes, *Spells of Enchantment: The Wondrous Fairy Tales of Western Culture,* for examples of a wide variety of European literary fairy tales.[21] Before going on to detailed analyses of a few of these literary fairy tales (which will be undertaken in chapter 6), we will survey in the next two chapters examples of fairy tales as they have circulated in oral tradition.

4

Fairy Tales with Male Protagonists

To illustrate further the generic characteristics identified in the introductory chapters and to suggest how gender influences fairy tales, we will undertake in this chapter an analysis of two selected fairy tales with male protagonists, "Three Hairs from the Devil's Beard" (AT 461) and "Faithful John" (AT 516). Both are examples of the middle and largest category of fairy tales, that is, tales for and about postpubescent adolescents. Both tales have ordinary protagonists who have no special abilities. The hero of "Three Hairs from the Devil's Beard" is born with a prophecy that he will marry the king's daughter, but he benefits from the help of others in accomplishing that task and demonstrates no special skill of his own during his adventure. Even though the protagonist of "Faithful John" is a king's son, he has no unique talents; he relies on the help of his faithful servant to achieve his goals and actually seems somewhat slow-witted at times.

These protagonists engage in a quest that involves their interaction with the magical realm. This realm is presented not only as legitimately existing, but also as having an important influence on the quotidian world of the protagonists, and therefore by implication on the everyday lives of the audience members. Both of these stories end happily. The happy ending serves to illustrate the moral dominion of this magical realm and the benefits of living one's life in harmony with it. Thus, the magical or supernatural dimension is verified and affirmed by these stories. Finally, the themes of these tales concern the typical issues of reconciling hostile attitudes toward older males or father figures, winning a mate, and establishing a domain of one's own. Let us examine how each story exemplifies these characteristics.

"Three Hairs from the Devil's Beard"

"Three Hairs from the Devil's Beard" (henceforth referred to as "Three Hairs") is listed as tale type 461 in Aarne and Thompson's *The Types of the Folktale* (156–8), which identifies more than 500 versions of this tale as having been collected and cataloged in various folktale archives in Europe. For example, they cite 212 Irish versions and 176 Finnish ones. Unfortunately, however, the vast majority of these versions are largely inaccessible unless one is willing to take the trouble to travel to the archives and is fluent in the languages in which they were collected, which in this case would include not only Gaelic and Finnish, but also various other European languages. Aarne and Thompson also list some versions from the Americas, as well as some from as far away as China and Indonesia. Suffice it to say, the tale is widely popular.[1]

Perhaps the best-known version of this tale for English-speaking audiences is that found in the Grimms' collection. This version follows the essential plot as it is outlined in Aarne and Thompson's index. The story frequently begins with a prophecy that a newborn child or young man (frequently the son of peasants) will become the king's son-in-law. The king attempts to block this marriage, initially by trying to dispose of the baby; in the Grimm version, for example, the king abandons the child in a box that is set adrift in the river. The child is rescued by a miller, and nothing more is heard until the child reaches young adulthood. Once again, the child comes to the attention of the king, who attempts to dispose of him by requesting of the youth's parents that he carry a sealed letter to the queen. The letter orders the bearer's death. On the way, the youth stops in a dark forest at the hut of an old woman whose sons are thieves. The letter is opened by them while he is asleep, and they change the letter to read that he should be given the king's daughter in marriage. The youth is accordingly married, and when the king returns, he then assigns the youth one final task to keep his bride—he must bring back three hairs from the devil's beard. The youth undertakes this quest.

On his way, he is presented with various questions, to which he is asked to find the answers. For example, in the Grimm version, the people of one town wish to know why a fountain, which once produced wine, no longer produces even water; in a second they ask why a tree no longer produces its golden apples; and finally, a ferryman wishes to know how he can be freed from his duties. In other versions, some of the questions concern how a sick prince or princess may be healed, where a lost princess is, where a lost key is, how a water-animal can be freed from some annoyance, why the livestock die, and how a girl, avoided by suitors, can marry.

The youth finds the devil's home, usually by crossing a river, and is aided there by the devil's wife or grandmother. He is transformed into an insect (an ant in the Grimm version), so that when the devil comes home, he smells the human flesh but is unable to find the young man. When the devil falls asleep, the wife pulls out a hair and, each time the devil awakes, claims she was troubled by a puzzling dream. The devil provides interpretations of the dreams that correspond to the protagonist's questions: The fountain will not flow because a toad is sitting under a stone in the well; if it is killed the wine will flow again. The tree has a mouse gnawing at its root; if it is killed the tree will produce apples again. And the ferryman needs only to put the oar in someone else's hand, and he will be free. The young man takes the three hairs, answers the questions on his way home, and obtains large amounts of gold in return. The envious king attempts to imitate the protagonist's exploits and winds up condemned to row the ferryboat eternally.

This tale's conformance to the generic characteristics of the incorporation of a fantastic element, an ordinary protagonist, and a quest that is successfully completed is reasonably self-evident. The corroboration of the depiction of a thematic core concerning the hurdles and obstacles to maturation and the use of fantasy to affirm the primacy of the spiritual or magical domain, however, require some analysis and elaboration.

At the outset, the problem motivating the story seems overtly related to a conflict between a young man and a male of the preceding generation. While some literal-minded readers might be inclined to view this conflict as illustrating upper-class resistance to social mobility—the king's not wanting his daughter to marry a peasant—this reading is too narrow. While the narrative is indeed legitimizing a democratic impulse for upward mobility, this issue is subordinate to a more immediate and pressing concern confronting the protagonist—his relationship to a father figure. The social mobility theme does not account for the peasant father's action in selling his son nor for the role of the miller in raising the boy or that of the devil himself as the ultimate antagonist. But if we view all these older males as father figures, we see that they are simplistically divided into good but ineffectual fathers (the peasant and the miller) and evil and threatening fathers (the king and the devil). All together they dramatize the developing young protagonist's attitudes toward his father, and the story is about his attempt to come to terms with this relationship.

At the outset, the young man views his father as essentially good but weak: the peasant is the good side of the father who created the protagonist but is unable to protect him from the bad side of the father, the manipulative king. The king as the imposer of laws and authority is an appropriate figure to represent the authoritarian side of the father, the side that the maturing young man inevitably resents. That the miller fulfills the role of a good father figure is revealed by the fact that he adopts the young man and that he is a humble and unassuming figure whose function is to provide food by grinding the wheat, much like the peasant father who grew the wheat. Their roles in creating and nurturing the protagonist are in direct contrast to that of the king, whose chief function is to enforce the laws and impose restrictions upon the protagonist, and whose chief desire is to eliminate this presumptuous rival.

The ultimate quest to get three hairs from the devil's beard is the heart of the story, both dramatically, in terms of its narrative structure, and thematically, in terms of its symbolic significance. Looking at the devil as a father figure provides one explanation for this central symbol. The young man must undertake this journey, this quest, in order to confront his image of his father, an image that is hostile and intimidating, so intimidating that it threatens to prevent the young man from maturing and living his life successfully. The devil in this light is much like the giant in "Jack and the Beanstalk" (known in Aarne and Thompson as "The Boy Steals the Giant's Treasure," Type 328). Both are ogreish giants who smell human flesh and wish to eat up the young boy. The eating may be seen accordingly as a metaphor of psychological domination and perceived parental aggression, rather than a literal reference to cannibalism.

The quest to confront this devil, then, is a quest to face up to the intimidating image of the father, which is this young man's greatest anxiety. The ambivalent attitude the young protagonist apparently possesses toward the father is reflected not only in this hostile older male from whom he must acquire three hairs and from whom he ultimately learns the secrets to life (the answers to the three questions), but also in the depiction of his original father's willingness to give up the son. The actions of these figures do not bespeak an entirely positive image of the father. Seeing the devil as a father figure also helps to explain the bizarre object of the quest, that is, to acquire three hairs from his beard. (This quest, and indeed the whole tale, resembles the story of Culhwch and Olwen in *The Mabinogion,* where Culhwch must obtain the prerequisites to be able to trim his prospective father-in-law's hair, in order to obtain permission to marry the daughter.) If we view the beard as a symbol of virility, then the young man's goal is to acquire some of that virility for himself, to procure at least the outward vestiges of manhood. The reason the young man is on the quest in the first place is that he wants to keep his bride, to maintain his sexual identity as her husband. Thus, the young man is learning to recognize and assert his own sexual feelings and identity by undertaking the quest.

This sexual development is intimated in the preceding adventure, when the young hero carries the letter to the king's castle. He does not consciously recognize the extent of the latent hostility existing between the king and himself (a hostility that may be regarded as primarily originating in the young man himself), inasmuch as he carries the message without realizing its contents. The episode in the forest, then, may be seen as a preliminary exploration of his subconscious feelings, following Campbell's theory that the journey into the dark forest is a metaphoric exploration of the protagonist's own unconscious. The young man falls asleep while at an old woman's hut, thus venturing even further into the unconscious mind. And in this hidden unconscious realm what he discovers is his other self, a multifaceted personality that lives in opposition to the king, represented appropriately by the woman's thieving sons, who are young men like the hero and whose thieving is in direct opposition to the king's law (much like Robin Hood's). What this other side of himself reveals (but only to the audience) is the existence of hostile feelings between the king and himself, the contents of the message that he carries but does not yet consciously recognize. (The feelings about the father are projected onto the father, making him the aggressor and guilty party in the conflict, which explains why it is the father figure who apparently bears the ill will exclusively.) In contrast to the problematic relation with a father figure plaguing the protagonist, the relation to a mother figure is very positive, given the evidence of the assistance of the thieves' mother here and the devil's mother later in the story. One might even interpret the thieves' situation with the mother as having an oedipal significance, an unconscious impulse the young man rejects in favor of marrying the king's daughter.

In addition to exposing his subliminal anxieties about the father figure, the representatives of his unconscious, the thieves, also perform the function of revealing his true desires. It is they who first suggest that the young protagonist wants to marry the princess. It is fitting that the young man's desire to marry the princess be first acknowledged in this unconscious realm where that feeling originates. The point of the narrative is to bring to conscious awareness the underlying feelings of the protagonist's unconscious, in this case, both his antagonism or ambivalence toward the father and his desire for a mate.

The reason the story does not end once the protagonist marries the princess, as it does in many other fairy tales, is that the hero has not yet confronted directly his true feelings about the king or the princess. In this episode, although these feelings are at least acknowledged sufficiently to influence his actions, that is, to promote his getting married, they remain unconscious. Although he achieves this marriage upon arriving at the castle, he has not completed the task of consciously recognizing and affirming the truth of either of his most significant and deep-seated feelings. The extent of the resentment toward the father still remains hidden in the disposed letter, and the desire for the daughter has been camouflaged by the pretense that he married her only because the thieves changed the letter to make it the apparent order of the king. The young man still has not openly acknowledged his true feelings, nor has he taken ultimate responsibility for his actions.

The quest to confront the devil is an attempt to accomplish both of these objectives. By completing the quest he demonstrates both his desire for the young lady and his willingness to face the father's awful image. The related goals of explaining why the fountain does not flow, why the tree does not produce, and why the ferryman is trapped are all related to this objective of self-awareness and self-assertion. Their connection is revealed in the answers to the problems. The fountain and the tree have something beneath the surface blocking their functionality, just as the young protagonist's unconscious anxieties are gnawing at his psyche and preventing him from living a successful and satisfactory existence. The lesson of the solution to these dilemmas is that a small unrecognized problem beneath the surface can interfere with the whole process, and therefore, the young man must learn to look inward and beneath his surface impression of things. He must recognize the root causes and influences in his own being and eliminate the negative agents that interfere with the proper operation of his life. His little nagging doubts and fears, represented by the mouse and the toad that block the fountain and the tree, must be acknowledged and removed.

These dilemmas also suggest another basic theme informing this narrative: the protagonist's confrontation of spiritual angst. The fountain and the tree are metaphors of the cyclical nature of life, of its ability to restore and renew itself. Their interrupted functioning suggests something is preventing the young protagonist from seeing the world as having or fulfilling its capacity for self-renewal. The hostility of the father figure, the intimidation of the preceding generation, apparently is perceived as a threat sufficient to disrupt the procreative and reproductive cycle. Inasmuch as the continuation of the authority and dominion of the king does represent an explicit effort to prevent the young man from marrying and having children with the daughter, then indeed this threat does seem to be interfering with the procreative urge and cyclic renewal of the universe.

The solution to the dilemmas, both psychological and spiritual, is found in the transcendent wisdom acquired in the supernatural realm from the devil himself, who may be seen not only as a father figure reluctantly imparting this secret wisdom to his son, but also as a cosmological figure of the greatest proportions. The magical nature of this realm and of the wisdom acquired is revealed in the magical transformation the protagonist must undergo in order to be capable of receiving this knowledge. He is changed into an ant or other form of insect and is hidden in the dress folds of the devil's mother. Furthermore, the answers are extracted from the sleeping devil through the ruse of awakening him by pulling out a hair each time. The connection between the hairs and the secret knowledge suggests that this knowledge is part of the devil's (and thus father's) power; it is, in fact, the secret of their virility or sexual power, and when the young man possesses it, he will be able to escape the dominion of the preceding generation. (See Ernest Jones, *Essays in Applied Psychoanalysis,* for a discussion of the symbolic significance of hair in folklore.)

The real-world potency of this secret wisdom—acquired in a supernatural realm from fantastic figures by the hero in another shape—serves to illustrate the importance of the transcendental or magical plane of existence, a plane that the narrative is indirectly encouraging its audience members to believe in and take seriously. While it is otherworldly—in one respect clearly separate from the quotidian realm in that the hero must not only undertake a long journey to experience it, but must cross a river guarded by a boatman under a magical curse—it nonetheless is efficacious in its ability to provide answers to the dilemmas of the quotidian world and meaning for the activities and events of everyday life. Thus, the fantasy serves to affirm a belief in things transcendental, magical, and supernatural and suggests that this mythical dimension can provide the solution to the spiritual angst experienced by the hero and, by extension, the audience.

Part of the dilemma confronting the protagonist is the philosophical assumption underlying the actions of the king. Not only does the king represent a projection of the young man's resentment of an authority figure and corresponding sense of an essential enmity existing between the two, the king also represents an example of selfish and self-centered behavior, an ethical and philosophical stance to which the young protagonist himself is also to some extent inclined by nature. He may be said to be projecting onto the king his own childish egotism, and the narrative serves to illustrate the impropriety, the very impiety, of such a philosophical outlook. The problem with the king's perspective, which represents a temptation with which the young hero is wrestling and a behavioral model that he must reject, is that such self-centeredness and preoccupation with self-aggrandizement and self-perpetuation is inherently doomed to failure. The inappropriateness of this outlook is confirmed by the king's fate—he is doomed to ferry the boat back and forth across the river. The answer to the third dilemma thus serves to reveal the philosophical dead-end of solipsistic self-centeredness. Much like the fate of Sysiphus in having to roll a rock eternally back up the hill, the king must engage in a monotonous and meaningless repeated action because his worldview is too self-preoccupied. If all the world is measured in relationship to the self, if no higher and transcendental powers and values are acknowledged, then life is reduced simply to a stage in which the individual acts out his egotistical desires. The world becomes a banal place, an existential wasteland, without the possibility of mystical epiphany. Thus, the affliction of the land, the barrenness of the fountain and tree, is linked to the spiritual barrenness of the land of the fisher king in the legend of the Grail quest. Without a vision of and a belief in things higher than ourselves, higher than the individual protagonist, life becomes empty and repetitious, leading nowhere except the grave. Not only is each life a dead-ended proposition in such a philosophical outlook, but each new life is simply another repetition of this dead-ended pattern.

Thus, the king's fate is a dramatic corroboration of the inadequacy of his spiritual perspective. The young man avoids this philosophical pitfall of entirely self-serving self-promotion by accepting the advice of the devil, not to grasp too firmly the oar of our existence. (That the devil gives this advice reveals his role as an outwardly intimidating father who actually possesses vital wisdom about life.) The king cannot let go of the oar because he essentially does not want to; his egotistical perspective inevitably encourages him to attempt to manipulate and control events around him and see everything in relation to himself, rather than to rise above the self and see things in relation to a higher and transcendental order. The protagonist's exposure to and incorporation of the magical realm enables him to escape the trap of solipsistic existentialism.

Thus the fantastic element in "The Three Hairs" promulgates a philosophical vision of the ultimate primacy of things mystical, magical, and mythical. The gold that the young hero acquires represents both a reward for having an appropriate appreciation for things magical and a metaphor of the spiritual wisdom he has brought back with him. It is fitting that he should tell the king, as he does in the Grimms' version, that the gold is as common as sand in the devil's realm, for indeed it is the coin of that realm. The spiritual wisdom the young hero achieved in the other world is a wisdom that is gold for this world, and it is a golden wisdom that can only be acquired in that mystical and nonconscious realm of awareness. According to this tale, what appears as meaningless and ordinary as sand to our rational and quotidian eyes, is in reality the golden essence of life when viewed with the eyes of the unconscious, with the inner insight of spiritual faith. The inner vision is what enables us to view existence not as possessing a soul-deadening sameness and valuelessness, not as an hourglass inexorably measuring the finite sands of our brief and pointless existence, but instead as an ongoing cycle of eternal regeneration, whose every particle is a minute inflection of the pure and perfect essence that is the divine cosmos, to see the day-to-day experiences and minutiae of life as the golden reflections of a higher existence.

In sum, "Three Hairs" exemplifies the basic characteristics of the fairy tale genre. It uses the formal techniques of an ordinary protagonist who successfully completes a fantastic quest in order to convey certain fundamental lessons about the maturation of the protagonist, in this case an adolescent hero, and about the essentially transcendental nature of the universe.

"Faithful John"

"Faithful John" is listed as tale type 516 in Aarne and Thompson, and they cite approximately 500 versions that have been collected and classified as fitting this tale type. More than 200 reside in Irish archives, and the other 300 versions are spread out through European archives and collections from European settlements in the Americas. There are a dozen published versions in Spanish, German, Russian, Italian, and Czechoslovakian, but only a few English translations, one of which is found in the English translation of the Grimms' collection.[2]

The basic plot of this fairy tale concerns a young man (generally a prince) whose father passes away and leaves the young man in the care of a faithful servant (hence the Grimms' title, "Faithful John") or a brother or foster brother. Either through a dream or through violating an injunction left by the father not to look into a forbidden room, the young man sees the image of a beautiful young woman and immediately falls in love. With the assistance of the servant or brother, the young man successfully finds and woos the young maiden. As in the Grimms' version, the servant may help the hero lure the princess on board a ship and then spirit her away. Or else, the servant or brother may help the young man steal into the princess' presence by dressing in women's clothes or by using a secret underground passage, or simply woo the princess as the adviser of the protagonist.

On the return voyage home, the protagonist encounters a variety of perils, including being offered poisoned food, poisoned clothing, or a magical horse, meeting some robbers or a drowning man, crossing a stream or passing through a door, having the princess faint after dancing, or having a snake enter the bridal chamber. Sometimes these perils are arranged by the father of the princess, or the protagonist's father or stepmother. The servant overhears some birds talking and learns about the upcoming perils, but he also learns that if he tells the prince, he will be turned to stone. The servant intervenes in each of the perils—for example, shooting the enchanted horse that threatens to abduct the prince, burning the poisoned cloak that threatens to burn the prince, and so forth. Each time he incurs the wrath of the prince until on the final intercession (which generally involves touching the princess in some way, such as drawing three drops of blood from her breast to revive her after fainting from excessive dancing), the prince condemns the servant to death, whereupon he tells the prince everything and is turned to stone.

The prince subsequently learns that he can restore the servant's life if he smears the statue of the servant with the blood of his children, or, in some versions, if he undertakes a long journey and acquires a magic remedy. The prince fulfills the conditions of the servant's reanimation, and in turn the servant demonstrates his gratitude, for example by resuscitating the prince's children.

Like all fairy tale types, this narrative has a thematic core underlying its basic plot and its various versions. This thematic core concerns, as it usually does in tales of adolescent heroes, the protagonist's maturation. In this tale, the maturation involves the acquisition of a mate (the search for and marriage to the princess) and the resolving of attitudes toward the father (the relationship to the faithful servant), in particular the internalizing of the moral code that the father embodies.

In the Grimms' version, the problematic relation to the father is intimated in the introductory episode, when the father on his deathbed calls his faithful servant to him and says, "Most faithful John, I feel my end approaching, and have no anxiety except about my son. He is still of tender age, and cannot always know how to guide himself. If you do not promise me to teach him everything that he ought to know, and to be his foster-father, I cannot close my eyes in peace" (43). The father's lack of confidence in his son is suggested in this passage, while Faithful John's role as a substitute father figure is directly confirmed. Faithful John's task is to teach the son all he *ought* to know, to help him learn how to *guide* himself. The emphasis is on the ethical and moral instruction that Faithful John is to impart, which implies the corresponding lack of a strong moral code in the prince. The father furthermore forbids the servant from showing the young man the picture of the princess of the Golden Dwelling, for, "If he sees that picture, he will fall violently in love with her, and will drop down in a swoon, and go through great danger for her sake, therefore you must protect him from that" (43). This passage reveals both the inclination toward emotionality in the young man (he indeed does fall into a faint when he sees the picture) and the overprotectiveness of the original father (he tries to prevent the exposure of his son to this challenge, rather than finding a strategy for helping his son to cope with it). In contrast, the faithful servant accedes to the young man's burning desire to explore the forbidden chamber and then works to help him master what he discovers there. The servant represents a more flexible and sympathetic father figure who gives the young man some credit and undertakes to support and assist him in his decisions. Thus, the death of the king and his replacement by the faithful servant represent the evolution of the son's attitude toward his father; the new father figure is an accommodation to the developing maturity and autonomy of the young man.

The exposure to the image of the princess, either in the forbidden chamber or in a dream, suggests strongly the young man's exploration of his unconscious feelings. The image either comes from his dreams, which is the voice of the unconscious, or is kept locked up in a room, which corresponds to his locked-up desires. In either case, once he sees the picture, his emotions, his passion, take over, and he falls violently in love with her, just as the first father figure predicted—the authoritarian king, who, while benignly having his son's interests at heart, does not think highly of the youth. Thus, the essence of the young man's dilemma is to determine an appropriate balance in the conflict between emotion, passion, and desire, on the one hand, and proper behavior, morality, and ethical responsibility, on the other. Faithful John represents a model of morality that the young man has literally inherited from his father, his conscience as it were. Faithful John follows Freud's reality principle: he is concerned with cause and effect and the consequences of actions, and thus he is pragmatic in his orientation. Appropriately, the faithful servant does indeed know how to woo the princess. In contrast, the young man follows the pleasure principle; he wishes only to satisfy his burning desire to possess the beautiful maiden but does not know how to accomplish this goal.

The method the servant employs to obtain the princess, however, suggests that he is practical and clever (luring her onto a merchant ship by enticing her with golden wares, in other words, exploiting the essential curiosity and materiality of human nature, demonstrating he knows how to attract and manipulate the opposite sex) but the fact that he then abducts her calls into question the refinement of his moral values. In other words, while the servant represents an incarnation of the father's morality for the son, it is, at this point, an incomplete and immature moral sense. The abduction (in contrast to the fairy tale of "The Cat as Helper" [AT 545], where the magical helper fools the king into giving the hero his daughter and half his kingdom) suggests that, from the young man's perspective, there is something faintly inappropriate about what he wants to do, that it must be done in opposition to social codes of behavior. The stealing of the princess is a giving in to the desires of the young man without reconciling them or accommodating them to the prevailing moral standards.

The abduction also suggests that the young man cannot fulfill the role of an appropriate suitor, perhaps because he does not regard himself as qualified for that task. Sometimes the protagonist secures admittance to the princess by dressing as a woman. This motif also intimates the incompleteness of the young man's development. He does not yet see himself as fulfilling the role and image of an adult male. This is why the story does not end with the acquisition of the princess, as many fairy tales do. The problem intimated at the start of the narrative, the young protagonist's inability to reconcile his sexual desires and his moral conscience, still remains. In this episode, he explores and acknowledges his unconscious desire, as suggested, for example, not only by the journey that he undertakes to see her (which, in Campbell's monomyth, would be interpreted as a journey into the unconscious mind), but also by his use of an underground passage to see the princess, that is, his venturing beneath the surface into the hidden realm of the mind. These desires had been up to this point repressed in the locked room. Now he learns what it is that he desires, and he gets what he wants (the princess), both of which events represent a step forward in his psychological development, but he does not successfully integrate these desires with the prevailing moral code. Because he abducts the princess, he apparently still regards his sexual desires as existing outside of or in opposition to the social order.

The perils that the protagonist encounters on his return home exemplify the nature of the lingering problem facing the hero. In the Grimms' version, these perils include a horse that will carry the hero away should he mount it, a bridal garment that will burn him if he wears it, and the fainting of his bride while dancing after the wedding. As a powerful beast, the horse symbolizes the young man's own animal instincts, which are threatening to carry him away. These instincts must be checked by the moral side, the servant, or else they may lead the young man to lose himself. The servant thus shoots the horse, much to the hero's dismay. Similarly, the bridal garment that burns is an image of the sexual passion aroused by the upcoming marriage, and once again the threat is that this passion, this raw emotionality, will be self-destructive. The servant throws the beautiful garment into the fire, once again provoking the protagonist's anger. The young man does not understand why he needs to keep his instinctive and sensual inclinations in check. To him they are appealing and unthreatening. To the conscience, however, they represent a temptation into self-indulgence that would be ultimately destructive. Thus, the servant, acting the role of the conscience, intercedes. The fact that the young man does not understand why reveals the extent of his immaturity. The servant is acting on the basis of unconscious wisdom (the revelations of the birds who are agents of mystical or esoteric knowledge), in other words, principles inherited from the father but not consciously recognized or empirically verified as yet by the young man. The young man must come to understand and accept the wisdom of the faithful servant.

The final challenge in the Grimms' version involves the fainting of the princess after dancing at the wedding. The dancing would be metaphoric of the anticipated physical intimacy following the marriage ceremony; it is in essence a ritualized metaphor of sexual intercourse, performed between two consenting adults and generally leading to sexual arousal when the dancers are romantically inclined or physically attracted to one another. The problem here is that the heroine gets overexcited, such that she faints, once again giving in to passion to such an extent that she risks injury. (Alternatively, the fainting might be read as an indication that the sexual passions of the prince have frightened her.) The servant's intervention takes the form of drawing three drops of blood from her right breast and spitting them out. The folkloric perception, particularly in medieval medicine but even lingering today, that the letting of blood somehow cools the passions and restores balance to the body explains the servant's actions: he is trying once again to keep the passion under control. In other versions of this fairy tale, the final peril concerns the entrance of a snake into the bridal chamber, which the servant must kill before it injures the prince and his bride.

The traditional associations of the snake with masculine sexuality suggest, once again, that unchecked desire poses a threat to the young couple.

Another related way to read this motif, as well as the preceding motifs and the overall action, however, is that the tale is not just offering a psychological lesson about balancing the instinctive and moral impulses in our natures, but is also suggesting a pragmatic and philosophical lesson about what constitutes the basis for a successful and enduring relationship between a man and a woman. The snake's threat might not be just that the young man's uncontrolled passion might frighten or alienate his new bride; rather, it might be suggesting that sexual passion should not be the only or primary motivation for marriage—that a marriage based solely on sexual desire is unhealthy and doomed to self-destruction. In other words, if sexual pleasure is the sole purpose of conjugal union, that union is built on sand; it will disintegrate as soon as the passions fade. This lesson is entirely congruent, however, with the psychological lesson about the necessity of controlling our impulsive instincts and emotions; it merely extends that lesson to a logically related social implementation.

In the course of saving the princess, either by drawing the blood or killing the snake, the servant touches the prince's wife. The protagonist, however, does not understand or agree with this action, and his annoyance with his servant and with the moral balance that Faithful John is trying to maintain results finally in the hero's condemning the servant to death. Ironically, while it is this familiarity with the queen that is ostensibly Faithful John's transgression—the fact that he violates social decorum and touches her—in reality, his transgression, from the young man's point of view, is that John, as an agent of morality, is interfering with the young man's inclination to indulge without restraint his desire to be with the princess physically, that he is not letting the protagonist touch her as he wants. Faithful John's actions are in direct opposition to the action of the dancing and the snake, in which the prince wishes to possess the heroine. Faithful John, in contrast, wishes to protect and restore her to herself. The young man cannot see the need for restraining his passions (either in the form of the dancing or the snake), which to him seem simply a source of pleasure. Thus, the condemning of the servant would suggest the young man wishes to relieve himself of the burden of having a conscience.

The young man cannot eliminate his moral side quite that simply, however. First, the servant is given the opportunity to tell his story, and when he does, the young hero realizes the legitimacy of Faithful John's behavior, and correspondingly, the value of the unconscious wisdom upon which the servant has been acting, and he repents his decision. In other words, he changes his mind about the importance of the role of the conscience in his life. But he apparently still does not have a genuine appreciation for the vital nature of the conscience: although he now wants to keep the servant around, he is able to do so only as a statue, as a stone monument to the moral code of behavior that he knows he should exemplify. His commitment to the moral principles that the servant represents, the ethics inherited from the father, is strong, but it is external and impersonal. He still needs to revivify those principles and made them vital and real for himself.

The servant's turning to stone and his ultimate resuscitation are further examples of the complex symbolism that is inherently a part of the genre of the fairy tale. That the servant would be turned to stone for revealing the reasons for his action would appear on the surface illogical. Generally in fairy tales, the relating of one's experiences and bringing to conscious awareness the motivations for one's actions lead to the redemption and restoration of the protagonist, for example, in "The Speaking Horsehead" (AT 533), where the protagonist tells her story to a stove and is restored to her rightful place, or in "The Dragon-Slayer" (AT 300), where the protagonist's claims are acknowledged when he tells the entire court how he killed the dragon and removed its tongue. Of course, in this tale, it is the servant and not the protagonist who does the relating, and as a consequence, the servant is turned to stone. This is exactly the point: the protagonist has not fully realized and integrated into his own psyche what the servant represents. It is the servant who knows and speaks; the hero must ultimately come to a similar understanding himself.

This essential detail reveals the thematic significance of this part of the tale. If the servant represents the conscience of the protagonist, then it would seem that the young man still does not have a good and healthy relationship with it. The young man initially did not understand the rationale of the servant, the logic of his conscience. When that rationale is articulated, however, the conscience becomes, as it were, petrified. The servant's being turned to stone would signify a codification of the moral values inherited from the father into a fixed and rigid set of rules. Now that it has been explained directly to the young hero, he understands in an external way the importance of his moral side, which now has come to dominate his life. This interpretation would seem to be indicated by the way the prince treats the statue of his servant. Rather than discarding it, as the speaking horsehead is discarded once it has been cut off in the tale of that name, thus allowing the serving girl to indulge her immoral impulses with the prince, the young man has the statue placed next to his bed. Discarding and ignoring the symbol of the conscience would suggest that the conscience is no longer functioning for the serving girl in "The Speaking Horsehead": she is living an id-oriented and self-indulgent existence. However, in "Faithful John," having the statue next to his bed would suggest that what it represents has become of central importance to the prince; the servant's (and thus implicitly the father's) stern moral presence is dominating the hero's life, even in the bedroom. It is as though he has adopted the moral codes externally and socially, fulfilling the expectations of his father, without really knowing and believing in them on a personal level.

This need to internalize and vitalize his morality is revealed in the protagonist's repeated desire to restore his servant to life: "Ah, if I could but bring you to life again, my most Faithful John" (50). And the servant's response in the Grimms' version is, "You can bring me to life again if you will use for that purpose what is dearest to you. . . . If you will cut off the heads of your two children with your own hand, and sprinkle me with their blood, I shall be restored to life" (50). In order to see the metaphoric morality implicitly conveyed by this grisly request, we must first get past the realistic image of infanticide. The story certainly is not encouraging parents to kill their children. The fact that these children are immediately brought back to life suggests that the transformation they undergo is one of perception or attitude, not of essence or physical existence. The father's attachment to his children is being fictionally recalibrated with respect to his com-

mitment to Faithful John and what he represents. It is the protagonist's preexisting emotional and moral imbalance that neces-
sitates his drastic and vividly dramatized recalibration. One general reason the sacrifice of what is nearest and dearest to the hero
is necessary to bring back Faithful John appears to be that the
hero must give up his most personal and cherished values in
order to make room for and accommodate these new values. The
hero cannot make Faithful John's (and implicitly his father's) values and principles his own without, to some extent, giving up
what he presently values. On a more specific level, these children are the products of his passion and physical relationship
with his wife, and his loving relationship to them once again represents the protagonist's preference for the instinctive and emotional side of his personality. He must learn to balance his love
for his children with an appreciation for morality. Appropriately,
having children intensifies the need for a balance between emotion and discipline in one's values and actions.

In other versions, the protagonist must obtain a remedy for
the servant and must undertake a long and arduous journey in
order to accomplish this task. Much as in "The Three Hairs," the
hero does not complete the task of self-realization and integration of the parts of his personality in his first journey; in both
cases, the heroes obtain their heart's desire, their bride, but still
have to undertake another quest to achieve complete happiness
and peace of mind. In these other versions of "Faithful John," the
fact that there still exists a problem is revealed in the idea that
Faithful John is sick or magically enchanted. The need for a remedy implies that all is not well in the hero's world. He needs to
venture into another realm, either the realm of the unconscious
or the realm of the supernatural, to restore a healthy balance to
his world.

The efficacious nature of this other realm is revealed by the
magical ability of the remedy to restore life to Faithful John and,
in the Grimms' version, to the children. The blood is symbolic of
the essential life force with which the young hero is shown literally coming in contact. The blood sacrifice also suggests that the
young man is giving up some of his childish emotionalism in
order to restore his conscience to its rightful place of authority.
The benefit of this for the young man is not only that he has a
healthier and happier psychological balance, but also that his

relationship to his family members is renewed. His wife has been praying in church that somehow they could restore life to the servant. Her discontentment with the present state of affairs shows further evidence that the protagonist's superficial solution to the moral dilemma he faced—the balancing of desire and duty—by transforming John into a statue, representing an external and pro forma adherence to the moral standards inherited from his father, is not sufficient for an entirely happy existence. It is functional—the protagonist does have a wife, children, and a social position—but it is somehow empty and artificial. It lacks the inner spiritual affirmation, the personal belief that would make his life seem whole and alive.

This transcendental acceptance of the propriety of morality (not on relativistic and pragmatic terms—that is, not based on the fact that it can get you what you want—but rather on absolute and eschatological terms—that is, because it is the way the universe is structured) corresponds to the philosophical significance of fairy tales. Fairy tales affirm a belief in the morality of the cosmos, and they simplistically depict a polarization of good and evil in the world in order to show the benefits of adhering to the good. The rewards gained by those who do good for the sake of goodness alone come in the form of supernatural miracles, the restoration of life to Faithful John and the children, which serves as cosmic testimony to the essential validity of this belief in moral propriety of the universe. Thus, this tale promotes not only a healthy psychological balance between two basic aspects of the personality, instincts and responsibility, but also a positive philosophical outlook that ties human moral behavior to the existence of higher laws in the universe.

5

Fairy Tales with Female Protagonists

While in folk tradition there appears to exist a reasonable balance between the number of male and female protagonists in fairy tales, in printed collections and in the minds of literate audiences, the female folk fairy tale seems to dominate. "Snow White" (AT 709), "Cinderella" (AT 510), "Sleeping Beauty" (AT 410), "Rapunzel" (AT 310), "Beauty and the Beast" (AT 425), "Little Red Riding Hood" (AT 333), and "Hansel and Gretel" (AT 327A) are just some of the most commonly remembered fairy tales that have female protagonists.

Perhaps one reason for this gendered preference in the genre has to do with the relative popularity of male versus female protagonists in related folk genres, particularly heroic legends. Given the disproportionate number of heroic legends that feature male protagonists, female audience members might have a greater need for role models in the fairy tale genre to compensate for the dearth of legendary heroines. This generic discrimination, however, reveals an implicit sexist bias in Western culture. The genres of legend and fairy tale are not equal. As our discussion in chapter 1 indicated, legends speak for a culture; their protagonists are culture heroes, embodying cultural values and ideals in overt ways. In contrast, fairy tales are more personal documents, speaking of individual needs and desires in familiar and quotidian contexts. While their language is fantastic—the language of the unconscious, as Bettelheim observes in *The Uses of Enchantment*—their subjects are the typical family relationships and maturational difficulties of average people. They have ordinary protagonists working through ordinary issues.

Accordingly, we can see a sexist bias evident when males are used predominantly to represent the ideals and models of behavior for a culture in its legends about itself, and females are relegated to the domestic roles of the family romances in fairy tales. This is not to say that the psychological concerns depicted in fairy tales are unimportant, or even less important, than the social models depicted in legends, but they cannot make up for the absence of such socially recognized role models. Try as Cinderella or Snow White might, they are not heroic figures who benefit the entire community through their actions the way Beowulf does. Their successes are inherently rather more personal and individualized, and thus they do not become social paragons or paradigms. They are emblematic of the ordinary person, which is the legitimate and valued subject of fairy tales, not of the exceptional person, which is the proper and, according to the worldview of those who create them, more socially elevated topic of legends.

Furthermore, not only is the relative popularity of female protagonists in fairy tales versus legends evidence of a sexist bias against the female gender, some scholars have argued that the content of fairy tales themselves promulgates prejudicial depictions of women; in other words, the treatment of fairy tale heroines might be regarded as unequal compared to fairy tale heroes.[1] The female protagonists are said to be relegated to passive roles, relying on others to provide guidance, motivation, and solutions to their problems. In many of the fairy tales, they are discouraged from speaking their minds or acting on their own initiatives. Their representation is stereotypical; they are associated with nature and primitive emotions and values, which the narratives ultimately depict as inferior to the civilized and rationalized representations of patriarchal roles and values. Even worse, in Sandra Gilbert's view, the social options available to women are capitulation to patriarchal conventions and values, which entails rejecting the mother and what she stands for, or outright social rejection (see the summary of her argument in chapter 7). Gilbert's readings of "Snow White" and "Allerleirauh" are powerful and persuasive, but they might be regarded as overly attuned to and thus overly stressing the theme of sexism in the tales. Although her analysis certainly provides evidence of sexist values in certain versions of fairy tales, the tales might be also regarded as offering some useful advice to its female audience members, not just coopting them into prescribed and invidious social roles.

In this chapter, we will undertake an analysis of two fairy tales with female protagonists, "The Speaking Horsehead" (AT 533) and "The Search for the Lost Husband" (AT 425), which includes the related subtypes of "Cupid and Psyche" (AT 425B) and "Beauty and the Beast" (AT 425C). We will assess not only the tales' conformance to the generic characteristics outlined previously, including the depiction of the theme of personal maturation, but also their degree of sexist bias in the expression of that theme.

Both of these tales have ordinary protagonists. Although the heroines of specific versions of both tales may occasionally be princesses, as, for example, in "The Goose-Girl" in the Grimms' collection or in "Cupid and Psyche" in the classical version of that narrative as told by Apuleius, they, like the prince in "Faithful John," are in no way gifted or special.[2] Each is a princess in name only and demonstrates no unique talents. The heroines of these two tale types are unambiguous characters with whom we can identify strongly. They find themselves beset by serious difficulties and embarked on significant journeys that will lead to the successful resolution of those difficulties. These journeys involve their interaction with a magical realm, and the incursion of the fantastic into their lives serves as a corroboration of the existence of the supernatural realm as well as a remedy for their psychological and spiritual ills. From a feminist perspective, the roles they ultimately fulfill do entail a subscription to the conventions of patriarchal society, but the extent to which these tales serve as a sexist primer versus a record of and a guide to coping with the extant sexism in the society must be determined from a closer examination of the evidence in both texts.

"The Speaking Horsehead"

"The Speaking Horsehead" is linked to "The Black and the White Bride" (AT 403) and "Little Brother and Little Sister" (AT 450), in that they all intrinsically involve the replacement or substitution of someone else for the heroine, either prior to her wedding or in her marriage. It is also closely related to the tale types known as "The Princess Confined in the Mound" (AT 870) and "The Little Goose-Girl" (AT 870A). All of these tales are, in turn, linked to the subgenre of tales of innocent persecuted heroines, which I define (in an essay in *Western Folklore*) as involving one or more of the three following basic acts: the persecution of the heroine in her parents' home, her persecution in her attempt to be married, and finally her persecution in her husband's home.[3] For example, in "The Speaking Horsehead," the persecution generally occurs during the heroine's wedding journey, when her serving maid forces her to change places with her. The other two closely related tales, "The Black and the White Bride" and "Little Brother and Little Sister," also offer instances of the heroine's being replaced on her way to be married. In addition, they sometimes depict the heroine's being replaced after she is married, frequently after her child is born; for example, she is thrown with her daughter into the water or transformed into a bird or a fish.

The value of seeing these connections is that we may understand "The Speaking Horsehead" in its larger context, not just in the context of the typical general narrative pattern of this fairy tale type as reflected in its various versions, but in the context of other tale types in which heroines experience the same kind of treatment as the heroine of this tale. The substitution of the bride or wife is a very common motif in these tale types, and thus it seems to speak to some broad underlying issues that concern a significant part of the audience for these tales. Perhaps an analysis of the specific details of "The Speaking Horsehead" will help us to understand these thematic resonances better.[4]

The version entitled "The Goose-Girl" related in the Grimms' collection (404–11) corresponds to the basic summary of events in Aarne and Thompson's type index. A princess is on her way to get married. Her mother gives her a large dowry, including a handkerchief—on which are three drops of the mother's blood—

and a talking horse named Falada. The heroine develops an insatiable thirst on the journey, but when her maid-in-waiting refuses to fetch the water from a stream, the heroine three times gets down off her horse and drinks from the stream. Each time the handkerchief says, "If this your mother knew, her heart would break in two" (405). The heroine loses the handkerchief in the stream, and the waiting-maid then forces the heroine to change horses and clothes and swear an oath not to reveal this to the court. In other versions, the heroine is sometimes blinded.

At the court the waiting-maid is conducted upstairs, while the real princess is assigned to the menial chore of goose-girl, that is, tending to the geese. The waiting-maid then requests of her new husband that he have Falada's head removed, and it is done. The heroine requests of the axeman that the head be nailed to a doorway through which she passes each day, and it is done. Each time she passes, the horse chides her by saying, "If this your mother knew, her heart would break in two" (408). She continues on her way tending geese with a goose-boy named Conrad. She combs her hair each day in front of Conrad, and when he seeks to touch it, she calls forth the wind to blow his hat away until she has her hair bound up again. Conrad then reports this behavior to the king, who investigates. In other versions, the geese tell the king about the beauty of the goose-girl or about some identifying mark she possesses (such as a gold star on her forehead or her gold or silver hair that she keeps hidden). The king asks her to tell her story but she cannot, so he tells her to tell it to the stove. She crawls into the stove and pours out her heart, and the king overhears by means of a stove pipe. Sometimes she sings a song or has a conversation with her dog, which the king similarly overhears. The king has royal garments placed on her and orders a great feast. At the feast the waiting-maid is asked how she would treat someone who behaved in such and such a way to her master, and he describes her crime exactly. She replies that the person should "be stripped entirely naked, and put in a barrel which is studded inside with pointed nails, and two white horses should be harnessed to it, which will drag her through one street after another, till she is dead" (411). The king orders it be done to her, the princess marries the king, and "both of them reign over their kingdom in peace and happiness" (411).

Although there are some apparent sexist strictures in this tale, it also seems to concern itself with some basic lessons about the conflict between instinct and morality, much like "Faithful John." It also appears to depict anxiety about acquiring a mate. The substitution of a false bride is a fascinating motif that recurs in many of these related fairy tales. It apparently dramatizes a number of parallel concerns on the part of the young heroine. One concern seems to be an ongoing competition with a mother, inasmuch as many of the antagonists who are interfering with the heroine's acquisition of a mate are portrayed as mother figures. These motifs apparently reflect a lingering oedipal rivalry still afflicting the prospective bride. Sometimes, however, the antagonist is a sister. In this case, the issue seems to be sibling rivalry.

In a number of tales, such as "The Speaking Horsehead," the person who replaces the heroine is her servant or maid, who seems to be a second self with whom the heroine is in conflict. This motif suggests something other than an oedipal conflict is underlying and motivating the action. Not only is the antagonist in these versions not her mother, but, as in the Grimms' version, the young heroine is also portrayed as having a particularly positive relationship with her mother. In fact, her mother encourages her to mature and get married and even gives her a substantial dowry, quite the opposite of the typical representations of oedipally jealous mother figures in other fairy tales, such as "Snow White," where the mothers are depicted as wanting to remain the most beautiful women forever. Rather than representing an oedipal conflict, the motif of the evil waiting-maid may be read as representing the dark and crass side of the heroine herself, which emerges in response to the anxiety and uncertainty occasioned by the upcoming marriage. This interpretation of the role of the waiting maid explains why she wields such power over the princess. It is because the princess lets her because the maid represents a side of the princess that she is having difficulty controlling.

The story seems to concern the obstacles to marriage that may be afflicting or are likely to afflict young women, inasmuch as the difficulties ensue on the journey to be married and interfere with the marriage. The main difficulties apparently concern the young heroine's ambivalent attitude toward sex. In other words, she has been brought up to believe, as most young girls in

Western culture are taught, that sex is dirty and immoral, but now, when she becomes a young woman with new biological urges and a new social status, suddenly she is expected to participate in sexuality. She has to deal not only with the change in the apparent social attitude that sex is appropriate in her new role as woman, but also with her own hormonal and psychological impulses, which are now biologically prompting her to engage in sex. The heroine's maturation to womanhood is symbolically conveyed in the tale by the metaphor of the three drops of blood on the handkerchief. The blood represents menstruation and general awareness of the physicality and sexuality that are part of being human. It is entirely appropriate that the heroine acquires this awareness from her mother in the bedroom, in the tradition of confidential parent-child talks on the threshold of the adolescent's transformation into an adult. That her mother gives her the handkerchief stained with three drops of the mother's blood is not only a graphic dramatization of the child's innocence being indelibly altered by the mother's knowledge, but it is also an appropriate representation of the fact that the heroine indeed inherits her woman's body and sexuality from her mother. These new imperatives, social and physiological, represent a major problem for the heroine.

This conflicted attitude toward sexuality is illustrated in "The Speaking Horsehead" by the heroine's losing her position (on the horse Falada and correspondingly as the future bride) as a result of having sullied herself by lying on the ground in order to quench her "thirst," in other words, to satisfy her sexual appetite. Three times the heroine gets down off her horse to drink, and each time the handkerchief says, "If this your mother knew, her heart would break in two." The repeated imperatives to drink depict the unavoidable demands her body is making on her. Her physiological needs are forcing her to do something that she believes her mother believes is immoral. She literally gets down off her high horse to satisfy her craving. The handkerchief would symbolize the conscience of the young heroine, which she has acquired from her mother, but which she must discard, accidentally on purpose, when she feels it expects too high a standard of behavior from her.

The serving girl who takes her place is blithely unfettered by the moral qualms that appear to afflict the heroine. The substitution in this case may be seen as a split between the two selves of the heroine, in which the more instinctual, self-gratifying, impulse-oriented, and less moral side of the heroine takes over. The amorality of the substitute bride is revealed in "The Speaking Horsehead" when the new bride immediately goes upstairs with the prince and soon after requests the brutal slaughter of Falada, the talking horse. The idea that a different side of the heroine is taking over might explain why the prospective husband never notices that he is marrying not just someone else, but someone far crasser. Since the change is an internal and psychological one, it would would not be readily apparent to others. Otherwise, the deception is about as literally plausible and effective as the substitution in "Little Red Riding Hood" of the grandmother by the wolf. Any cognizant human being would notice a difference in a real-world situation. In the euphemistic realm of fantasy, however, for the sake of the plot and the underlying thematic symbolism, the ruse succeeds.

Another concern raised by this popular motif of the heroine's not being recognized by her husband or her husband-to-be is that of not having one's true worth appreciated. Inasmuch as the future and current husband seems not to be able to recognize the true heroine, he is not seeing her true self, her true value. Similarly, in "Cinderella" the future mate thinks of the heroine as merely a serving girl. In "The Speaking Horsehead" the husband mistakes the crass, immoral, and carnal serving girl for his true bride. In addition to depicting the heroine's not having her true worth appreciated, this representation may reflect as well the concern on the young woman's part that her husband wants her for the wrong reasons. This motif also reveals the flawed perspective and incorrect assessments made by male figures, which amounts to an antisexist revelation about the limitations of men. Inasmuch as the males are not shown to be inevitably right and infallible, paragons of moral judgment and perspicacity, but rather self-preoccupied and unperceptive, this characterization may be seen as a female commentary on male faults, which provides some (albeit small) evidence that an alternative perspective to the sexist, patriarchal point of view may be seen in fairy tales.

Notwithstanding the emotional turmoil reflected in the various motifs found in these related folktales of supplanted heroines, ultimately the tales demonstrate how the obstacles are overcome inevitably and naturally as the heroine weds her future mate. Various routes to the socially encouraged state of marriage are depicted in these tales of persecuted heroines. In "Snow White" and "Sleeping Beauty" the heroine is simply rescued from her catatonic condition by a prince who is attracted by her beauty or reports of her beauty. In contrast, in "Cinderella" and many of the other tales about substitute brides, the heroine must act to achieve her desire. She employs disguise and cunning to manipulate the prospective mate into recognizing and appreciating her. For example, in "The Princess Confined in the Mound" (AT 870), the heroine manages to reclaim her former lover by temporarily replacing her rival during the wedding ceremony because the rival is too pregnant to wear the wedding dress. The heroine talks to her horse, to the bridge, and to the church door. The prince overhears these monologues and when he asks the false bride later that night about the conversations, she cannot recall them. He realizes she is not the one he married and is not his true love. He restores the heroine to her rightful position.

In some of these tales, the heroine is restored by her virtue more than by her pluck. For example, in some versions of "The Little Goose-Girl" the heroine is recognized by a magic stone by the prince's bed that indicates the bride's chastity. The immoral substitute is exposed, while the purity of the heroine is confirmed. The preceding route emphasized the heroine's initiative and persistence, but this route rewards her for conforming to the social strictures regarding female virginity.

In contrast, in "The Speaking Horsehead" the heroine is restored to her rightful place once she learns to use her social skills and manipulate the opposite sex. The heroine each day undoes her hair and combs it in front of Conrad, her young companion, while they are tending geese. He is attracted to the shining hair and tries to touch it. She calls forth the wind to blow his hat away, and while he chases his hat, she binds her hair again. The flirtatious nature of the heroine's behavior reveals that she has mastered the art of courting. The heroine employs the sexual provocation of playing with her hair in order to entice her companion Conrad, but she does not let the sexual arousal get out of control. Before Conrad can violate social decorum, she reminds him of his place, which is symbolically conveyed by blowing his hat (his social image) off. That someone who is sexually aroused

would be realistically deterred by his hat blowing off is not particularly plausible; however, if the hat represented Conrad's
image of himself, his social persona, the heroine in calling forth
the wind to blow it away is reminding him of how his actions
might appear to others. In chasing the hat, Conrad is symbolically trying to preserve his social propriety. This concern sufficiently checks the young boy so that the heroine can maintain control
of the situation.

Her control leads Conrad to report the situation to the king,
who asks the heroine to explain why she talks to the horsehead
every day and teases Conrad. She says she cannot tell the king,
so he uses the ruse of the stove in order to overhear her story.
These colorful motifs illustrate the symbolic nature of fairy tales
and the way they figuratively depict the young woman's ongoing maturation. The stove functions nicely as a metaphor of the
heroine's mother. It metonymically suggests the mother's
domain, the home and hearth and kitchen, and her function, to
provide emotional warmth and sustenance. The heroine's crawling into the stove suggests a reconciliation with the mother, a
reconciliation that the tale shows is necessary to the heroine's
successful maturation and initiation into the role of mother and
mature woman herself. The heroine cannot complete her initiation into womanhood until she acquires an appreciation for her
mother. The heroine must reestablish a relationship with her
mother, must be able to talk to her as the heroine talks to the
stove; that the father hears things indirectly through the mother
is suggested by his listening at the stovepipe. She must accept
and assimilate her mother's moral code, the superego she has
inherited from her mother. In "The Speaking Horsehead" it is
the conflict between these demands of her inherited morality
and the id-motivated demands of her developing sexuality that
creates the heroine's major problem in the first place and leads
her to forsake her birthright and opt instead to regress into the
demeaning and undemanding role of a goose-girl.

According to the cultural logic of the story, the heroine must
accept what it is physiologically to be a woman, that is, to be able
to give birth. The image of the heroine crawling into the stove
aptly conveys this message by presenting the metaphor of gestation. The stove is not only the mother but also the mother's
womb. In returning to it, the heroine recaptures the closeness

and warmth of her relationship with her mother and anticipates her future role as mother. Being inside the stove is suggestive of pregnancy, much akin to the folk expression used to describe a pregnant woman: she has a bun in the oven. Thus, the heroine in acting out this event is confirming in a metaphoric way the philosophical justification for sexuality that can alleviate her moral qualms about engaging in sex. Because sex engenders life, it is not only morally proper, it is cosmically sanctioned.

Finally, at the banquet the king asks the false bride how to punish someone who acts in the manner that the heroine has described, and the maid unwittingly pronounces her own sentence, to be dragged by horses through the streets in a barrel with nails stuck through it until she is dead. The motif of the substitute bride passing sentence on herself is found in versions of "Snow White" as well. If the maid represents the childish and pleasure seeking id side of the heroine, the judgment reveals that this childish side nonetheless expects others to treat it fairly, even if it does not abide my moral considerations itself. The fact that the king enforces the moral code suggests that part of the social initiation of women in these stories is to encourage them to rely on and be reassured about the ability of society to punish its transgressors. This represents quite a contrast with male fairy tales in which the protagonists dispatch their own adversaries. There are versions of "The Dragon-Slayer" (AT 300), however, one of the most popular male fairy tales, in which the hero reports the crime of his adversary to the court or king, and the court or king determine the appropriate punishment. In contrast, there is at least one version of "Snow White" in which the heroine takes a gun and shoots her evil adversary herself. Thus, while there is a gender bias in these stories, it is not absolute, and the encouragement to rely on social justice is ethically admirable on the whole.

Metaphorically, the image of the waiting-maid being placed in the barrel serves as a graphic counterpoint to the image of the goose-girl crawling into the stove. Whereas the waiting-maid's justification and motivation for engaging in sex is personal self-gratification, giving into urges unreservedly, the goose-girl's justification for ultimately engaging in the sexual act of marriage is that it fulfills the cosmic imperative of perpetuating the race. Accordingly, the heroine's act is shown to lead to fruitful results;

analogous to the function of an oven, her womb will produce and nurture new life. In contrast, the waiting-maid is metaphorically placed in a sterile or barren womb, which is violated by repeated phallic penetrations as it is dragged all over town, a harsh critique of the moral and cosmological as well as the psychological drawbacks of indulging the self-gratification of one's impulses.

Thus we find that this fairy tale once more relies heavily on the analogical function of fantastic symbols to convey lessons about the maturation of its protagonist. These fantastic motifs may be seen as externalizations of unconscious fears and desires harbored by the protagonist. While there are certainly sexist strictures present in the related tales of persecuted heroines, there are also worthwhile lessons about coping with various anxieties occasioned by the process of growing up. In addition to dramatizing the theme of maturation through fantastic images, these tales also fulfill the other generic characteristics of presenting modest protagonists with whom we can identify and who undertake quests to solve the problems confronting them.

"The Search for the Lost Husband"

Another popular fairy tale with a female protagonist that exemplifies the essential characteristics of this genre is "The Search for the Lost Husband" (AT 425). According to Thompson's *The Types of the Folktale,* it includes two main related subtypes: "The Monster (Animal) as Bridegroom" (AT 425A; also known as "Cupid and Psyche," from the best-known classical version of that story by Apuleius) and "Beauty and the Beast" (AT 425C), from the French version told by Madame Villeneuve and subsequently retold by Madame de Beaumont.[5] Essentially, this tale is about the marriage of a young woman to a monster, who may be, in the different versions, a dwarf, bear, wolf, ass, snake, hog, hedgehog, frog, bird, or tree. Sometimes the story begins with an explanation of how the monster was created, for example, because of a hasty wish by his parents or because of a curse that has been laid on him. The focus of the story, however, is on the young woman and how she becomes involved with or engaged to this monster.

In the Grimms' version of "Beauty and the Beast," which is entitled "The Singing, Soaring Lark" (399–404), a daughter asks her father to bring back a singing, soaring lark. When the father attempts to capture the bird, a lion attacks him. In return for sparing his life, the lion makes the father promise to give the lion whatever first meets him on his way home. Of course it is his youngest daughter. The daughter complies with her father's promise and discovers that the lion is an enchanted prince who resumes his human form at night. In the French version told by Madame Villeneuve, the father promises his daughter to the monster in return for a flower his daughter asked him to get. In other versions it may be to pay a gambling debt, or otherwise to escape from some danger he has fallen into. In a Norwegian version collected by Asbjörnson, "East o' the Sun and West o' the Moon," a bear comes to the house and offers a father great riches if his youngest daughter will marry the bear.[6] The daughter initially refuses but ultimately consents to the match. In some versions of this fairy tale, she promises herself to the monster to recover stolen jewels or clothes or to escape captivity in a spring or well. Or she may actually seek out or accidentally discover this supernatural husband on her own.

After one of these introductory motifs explains how the heroine comes to live with the monster, the next significant episode concerns the heroine's violation of the monster husband's injunction. In the Grimm's version of "The Singing, Soaring Lark" the heroine insists that her husband accompany her to her sister's wedding, even though he warns her that if any candlelight should fall on him, he would be turned into a dove for seven years. Sure enough, a tiny ray of candlelight shines through a crack in the bedroom door, and the husband becomes a dove. In Madame Villeneuve's version, the husband cautions the heroine not to overstay her return visit to her family. When she violates this taboo, the monster nearly dies. In "Cupid and Psyche," as told by Apuleius and translated by Edith Hamilton, Cupid warns Psyche not to let her family persuade her to try to see him, but they nonetheless manage to persuade her to bring a lamp into the bedroom to examine him, as well as a sharp knife should he turn out to be a serpent. She finds a beautiful youth, but she inadvertently burns him with a drop of hot oil, and he flees. Similarly, in "East o' the Sun, West o' the Moon," despite the bear's warning, the heroine lets her mother persuade her to bring a candle into the bedroom to see what kind of man or monster sleeps with her at night. When she sees that it is a lovely prince, she falls in love with him, but when she tries to kiss him, she drops hot tallow on his nightshirt and awakens him. Because she violated the taboo, the bear must now marry a princess who lives East o' the Sun and West o' the Moon.

The main difference, according to Thompson, between the subtypes of this fairy tale is that in "Cupid and Psyche" and its related versions, the heroine must undertake a quest for her vanished bridegroom, which generally includes the heroine's accomplishing a set of tasks, whereas in versions of "Beauty and the Beast" the heroine disenchants the monster by means of a kiss or tears or an embrace without engaging in a search for him or undertaking a set of tasks. (Other forms of disenchantment include burning the animal skin the monster wears during the day or decapitating him.) However, Thompson lists "The Singing, Soaring Lark" as a version of "Beauty and the Beast," even though the heroine engages on a quest for her lost husband in that tale. In fact, the distinction between the two subtypes is not well maintained, and it seems reasonable to regard them as two versions of the same tale type, "Beauty and the Beast" simply being a popular abbreviated form. In essence, since the episode of the heroine's quest is one that commonly, but not invariably, occurs in versions of this fairy tale, the tale type should not be entitled "The Search for the Lost Husband" (as Thompson entitles it) but rather "The Monster (Animal) as Bridegroom," with "Beauty and the Beast" listed as a major variant in which the quest is omitted.

The Grimms' "The Singing, Soaring Lark" follows the main tale type and includes a quest. The dove tells the heroine that at every seventh step, it will let fall a drop of red blood and a white feather. She is to follow them for seven years, and then she will be able to release her husband, and they will be reunited. After seven years she is ready to rescue him, but he disappears. She then asks the sun, moon, and the night wind the whereabouts of her husband. The sun and moon do not know, but they give her a magic casket and a magic egg, respectively. The night wind consults the south wind, who tells her to go to the Red Sea, where her husband is a lion again and is fighting a dragon, who is an enchanted princess. She is further told to secure a reed that will disenchant the dragon and allow the lion to be victorious. She is then to swing herself and her beloved onto a griffin, and the bird will carry them home.

Although she follows these instructions carefully, when the dragon is conquered, the enchanted princess regains her human form and quickly takes the husband on her arm and seats herself on the griffin and carries him off. The heroine continues her quest until she finally finds where they are living together. She now uses the sun's magic gift, which turns into a dress as brilliant as the sun itself. With it she buys a night with the husband, but he is drugged and sleeps through the night. She then opens the egg and out come a mother hen with twelve chickens all of gold. She trades them to the false bride for a second night with her husband, and this time she intercepts the sleeping draught and her husband recognizes her. They escape on the griffin, and she remembers to let fall the nut given to her by the night wind, which turns into a tree on which the griffin may rest so that he can carry them all the way home. There, they find their child, who has grown tall and beautiful.

The Grimms' collection also offers another version of this fairy tale that presents the heroine as engaging in a quest for the lost husband. It is entitled "The Iron Stove" (571–7) because the heroine, in return for information on how to get home again after she becomes lost in the woods, promises herself to a king's son who has been bewitched by an old witch and shut up in an iron stove in a forest. Although she tries to have substitutes take her place, they cannot scrape a hole in the iron stove, so finally, she returns to free the king's son, who turns out to be "so handsome, and so brilliant with gold and with precious jewels, that her very soul was delighted" (573).

After she convinces the king's son to let her return to see her father, the heroine violates her betrothed's injunction not to say more than three words to her father. The iron stove disappears over glass mountains and piercing swords, and the king's son with it, so the heroine is unable to find him when she returns. She searches for nine days and finally climbs into a tree for protection from wild beasts. There she sees a light and, when she goes to it, finds a little old house inhabited by toads. When she tells the toads her tale, they offer her food and drink and then three large needles out of a great box, a plow-wheel, and three nuts. They are to be used to cross the glass mountain, the piercing swords, and a great lake in order to recover her lover. She uses the needles behind and before her feet to get over the glass mountain and the plow-wheel to roll over the piercing swords. Once she crosses the lake, she takes employment as a scullery maid in the castle where her beloved is living. He is about to become married, for "he thought that she had long been dead" (575).

The heroine opens the first of her magic nuts and finds a beautiful royal garment, which she trades to the bride-to-be for a night in the bridegroom's chamber. The false bride pours a sleeping draught into the prince's wine, so he does not realize the heroine is there. The servants, however, hear the heroine's tale and her weeping and tell the king's son about it in the morning. The same thing happens on the second night. Finally, on the third night, which is bought with a dress of pure gold, the king's son throws away the sleeping draught and recognizes his true bride. They get into a carriage, take the false bride's clothes, and return across the lake, the swords, and the mountain. When they return to the toad's house, "it was now a great castle, and the toads were all disenchanted, and were King's children, and full of happiness" (577). They remain in the castle, and "as the old King grieved at being left alone, they fetched him away, and brought him to live with them" (577).

As the synopses suggest, these versions are not only closely linked to each other, but also to other fairy tales of persecuted heroines. The last part of this last tale is frequently found in a subtype of "Cinderella" known as "The Dress of Gold, of Silver, and of Stars" (AT 510B). While that tale type begins with the traditional "Cinderella" episodes of the heroine's being victimized in her own home by a wicked stepmother or stepsisters, in the conclusion of that tale the heroine uses a succession of magically beautiful dresses to win her spouse, much as in "The Iron Stove," one of the Grimms' versions of "Cupid and Psyche." These coincidences reveal the fundamental link between these related tales. They are symbolic depictions of social and emotional crises faced by audience members. In particular, these tales appear to dramatize the central and apparently problematic experience of coming to terms with marriage. They begin with the meeting of the prospective mate, and then through the use of fantastic metaphors they chart the obstacles, difficulties, social expectations, and personal anxieties associated with adjusting to the institution of marriage. In this way they fulfill the generic characteristic of fairy tales of using fantasy to provide representations of developmental issues of interest to audience members.

In all these versions and tale types, magic or fantasy is central to the events. In "The Search for the Lost Husband" the enchantment of the monster bridegroom begins the tales, the violation of a taboo by the heroine leads to further magical enchantments, and finally the heroine must employ magic to reclaim the husband. The depiction of magic in the tale suggests it is not only a potent force in the world, but an efficacious one if used wisely and correctly. The heroine engages on a quest that brings her into closer contact with the magical realm, and she learns to appreciate and use the magic to her own advantage. Finally, the heroine is a positive figure with whom audiences can identify strongly, and her actions do appear to dramatize a theme of adolescent maturation, if we analyze closely the symbolic imagery of the tales.

We should acknowledge at the outset of such an analysis that this tale and these versions may be understood as symbolically conveying a variety of significant themes. Feminists would emphasize that the marriage contract the heroine is locked into is evidence of a patriarchal system in which the heroine, in Sandra Gilbert's words, is taught to "bury the mother, and marry the father" (see her analysis in "Life's Empty Pack" of "Allerleirauh," which is the Grimms' version of "The Dress of Gold, of Silver, and of Stars"). The fact that the grieving old father is brought to live with the princess and her husband in "The Iron Stove" (and no mention is made of the mother) would suggest that this conclusion is implicitly promoting the adoption of the moral value system represented by the father. This ending is very similar to the ending of George Eliot's *Silas Marner,* which is analyzed by Gilbert to show how the daughter redeems the father and affirms the social system by marrying and giving herself to someone just like her father.

Furthermore, the bear's emphasis in "East o' the Sun and West o' the Moon" that the heroine not let her mother take her aside and talk to her alone, since she will try to unduly influence the heroine, seems a fairly overt message to young audience members to reject their mothers and their mothers' advice in favor of the males' perspective. That following the mother's advice does lead to further difficulties, and the fact that it turns out the bear's curse is a result of a wicked stepmother, would apparently serve as explicit confirmation of the sexist lesson underlying this story—that women are untrustworthy as authority figures. Their "natural" and appropriate role is to be subservient to and guided by male authority. When they act on their own, they are perceived as being self-serving and destructive. The same lesson is suggested in "Cupid and Psyche" when the heroine takes the sisters' advice over the advice of Cupid and pays the price for it. It is interesting to note that in the tales where the heroine violates the husband's taboo by staying too long to be with her father (as in "Beauty and the Beast"), it is not a result of the father's suggestion, but rather a product of the heroine's giving in to her own emotions. Males do not offer bad advice in any of these texts; only females do. Thus these tales serve implicitly to sanction males as authority figures.

Alternatively, sociohistorians would focus on the fact that it is by using the dresses to buy nights with the king's son that the heroine gains her husband and social position. In other words, the tales are not only fostering a bourgeois or elitist social stratification and encouraging the heroine to want to attain the appropriate social stratum, but they are also promoting the materialistic and mercantile values that are the foundation of such a society. Not only does the story suggest a dowry is crucial for social advancement, but it also suggests that the heroine must learn how to use the dresses, the social artifacts, to succeed. In essence, the story teaches us that a proper appreciation for and crafty acquisition of superior material goods are the keys to social success. The fact that the dresses apparently have supernatural beauty and power may be understood as evidence of their psychological hold over those who view them. In other words, if beauty is in the eye of the beholder, then those who behold the beauty of these material possessions are enchanted by them.

While, to some extent, these social lessons do indeed appear to characterize the symbolic events in these fairy tale versions, they are part of a larger complex of developmental themes and philosophical lessons promulgated by the tales. One could overlook other, possibly more central or important, messages offered by these texts if one concentrated too heavily on these feminist and economic themes. There is basic textual evidence that seems to qualify both the feminist and economic messages.

Specifically, the heroines in "The Singing, Soaring Lark" and "The Iron Stove" are shown to be acquiring their power not from a masculine, patriarchal social system, but from the night wind and from an old toad who is referred to as "she" ("then *she* gave her, three things" [574; italics mine]). These crucial donor figures teach a lesson that is quite different from, even diametrically opposed to, the feminist and economic lessons. Rather than dramatizing the cosmic omnipotence and omnipresence of the patriarchal and mercantile social system, as, for example, the mythologies of Zeus and Yahweh do, these fairy tales suggest instead that the heroine should get in touch with and rely on some rather naturalistic and primitive powers or forces that are unseen in this world. If the night wind and the toads are embodiments of the divine or supernatural forces in the cosmos, they are not paternal or commercial gods. Rather, they are otherworldly and chthonic figures, denizens of a dark netherworld the heroine must journey to. They serve as moral guardians, correcting the injustices of this world—helping to repair the loss of the heroine's husband and to prevent the unethical attempt by someone else to marry her husband in her place. As agents of cosmic order and propriety, they illustrate the existence of powers and laws greater than society. They encourage metaphorically an appreciation for the unseen and apparently unimportant aspects of life: the night wind and the toads are things overlooked or taken for granted in this world. Ultimately, these tales, like all those in the fairy tale genre, encourage a belief in a supernatural power that will help the heroine attain her goals in this world.

It is true that succeeding in the social realm is a fundamental goal of the narrative and that complying with extant social conventions is stressed. The tales are conformist in that they do not advocate rebellious rejection of or even individualistic alternatives to the traditional marriage contract. As a matter of fact, they even link the marriage to the supernatural powers, in that it is the goal of those powers to foster marriage, thereby implicitly sanctioning it as a cosmically endorsed phenomenon. The worldview of these tales is quite narrow: marriage is the only appropriate option available to the heroine. The fact that these goals are socially defined, and accordingly are necessarily paternalistic and materialistic is, to some extent, a realistic reflection of and pragmatic accommodation to the influences of the social realm upon the heroine's quotidian desires and those whom she represents.

While the tales are realistically acknowledging the concrete and commercial nature of the heroine's desires and of society's expectations for her, they are not simply condoning and reinforcing those material wants. They subordinate those desires to a higher authority that is symbolically antithetical to the social goals; the night wind and the toads are not themselves embodiments of commercial success. What is elevated to divine or supernatural status is something quite different. They embody the power of nature, its most elemental and crude forces. It is an appreciation of these forces that separates the heroine from her competitors and that enables her to achieve her fondest wishes. While this moral force manifests itself in the world by providing concrete and material goods, what is superior about these goods is that they are "pure gold." In other words, these goods are not really comparable to other worldly goods; they completely outshine any ordinary materialistic human artifacts. The essential message is that materialism divorced from spirituality is insufficient and inadequate. Being in harmony with this supernatural dimension of the universe is what leads to successful participation in the commonplace aspects of life. The fundamental lesson of the tale, thus, is very spiritual and cosmological. Yes, the heroine must learn how to function in the social realm that she happens to find herself in and that social realm is distinctly patriarchal, but the story suggests that only by recognizing and communing with the magical elements in the universe will she truly succeed in the social realm.

These fantastic motifs may be read not only as providing spiritual instruction, as we have already discussed, but also as offering psychological lessons for their audiences. For example, why the prospective husband is magically transformed into a lion or locked up in a stove may be explained if we regard this tale as an illustration of the anxieties that accompany marriage. In this light, the transformation of the prospective husband makes perfect sense, for it reflects the heroine's attitude toward her prospective mate. In other words, if these tales dramatize the emotional qualms experienced by young women in contemplating marriage, then the various forms that the mate assumes may be explained as alternative representations of the various fears the heroine may have about him. For example, the serpent in "Cupid and Psyche," or the wild animal in "Beauty and the Beast," or the lion in "The Singing, Soaring Lark" may be seen as metaphors of the heroine's basic anxiety about the masculine animality or sexuality of her prospective mate.

The king's son in the stove is a complex image that may be read both from a psychological and a feminist perspective. Psychologically, the image of being locked in a stove embodies the heroine's fears about a mate; to the heroine, her mate seems hidden, mysterious, unreachable, and foreign. His curious stove disguise, however, does not conform to the traditional metaphoric externalizations of the heroine's anxiety about his virile and threatening masculinity, as do the motifs of the serpent or lion cited above. He is shrouded by an image associated with femininity, the stove. But like the bestial images, the image of the stove may be understood as a projection of the heroine's perception of her prospective mate imposed on him. It is she who is prevented from seeing the true king's son because of her anxieties about what he represents. The curse by the old witch may represent the lingering influence of the mother's morality or an oedipal threat, interfering with the heroine's ability to see and enjoy the appeal of the opposite sex. When she scrapes away the false illusions that block her vision, she finds that he is a handsome and brilliant youth who delights her very soul. Her own objections and fears were what had blocked her vision. Much like the goose-girl in "The Speaking Horsehead," she is trapped by her own doubts about sexuality and procreation, which are metaphorically suggested by the stove being a place of entrapment rather than a source of production. It is suggested also by the fact that each time the heroine is lost she wanders for nine days, evoking an association with gestation. Furthermore, in the story's conclusion, the toads become disenchanted and turn out to be king's children, which apparently confirms that procreation is the central issue of the narrative. Once the heroine is able to sort out and assert her feelings toward the husband (she is initially quite ambivalent about him), then marriage and children naturally follow.

Interestingly, this motif also suggests a feminist theme. By agreeing to marry him, the heroine frees him from the domination of the witch's curse. In other words, marriage serves as a mechanism of empowerment for the male, freeing him from motherly domination in a psychological context, and linking him to society and an order-making social role in a cultural context. Thus, these motifs, and the tales they are a part of, convey both psychological and social lessons. They are, like much art, complex documents communicating multiple and even contradictory messages simultaneously.

If, as we have suggested, the disguise of the prince may be seen as a projection of the heroine's anxieties about him in response to the prospect of marriage, then what gets her involved with him may be interpreted as a metaphoric expression of her feelings about a mate. Specifically, the fact that her request for a singing bird or beautiful flower is what leads to a relationship with the beast suggests that it is the heroine's own emotional yearnings that precipitate the involvement in the first place. That the heroine cannot have her emotional totem apart from the beast suggests that the two are inextricably linked. In other words, the heroine's emotional desires lead her to an age-mate of the opposite sex despite her ambivalent feelings toward such a figure and such a relationship. While the desire is reflected in the emotion-charged objects of beauty, the ambivalence is reflected in the way this prospective mate is represented as having an awesome and fierce guise, which threatens to interfere with the siblings and with her new relationship to her spouse. These tales stress the importance of the heroine's affiliating herself and her loyalties with her new husband at the expense of her childhood family, which perhaps might be regarded as a sexist affirmation of the male's centrality and the need of the female to renounce her prior attachments in favor of her new marital position. From a feminist perspective, the heroine is encouraged to give up her family and, like a piece of chattel, become "part" of the husband's clan. She must revise her notions of what constitutes her "family." Continuing to identify with her parents and siblings as her family is shown to be dangerous and dysfunctional. This message—in its severest form, that is, requiring her to reject her parents entirely—certainly has unpleasant sexist implications, but in a more pragmatic or limited application—that is, realizing that one's closest ties are now to the person one lives with—this lesson might still be regarded as having some emotional truth to it. The heroine does need to learn to put her relationship with her husband ahead of that with her parents and siblings.

The disappearance of the husband presumably suggests that the heroine is not quite ready for the relationship, perhaps because it conflicts with her existing social values and relationships. The partial disenchantment (the husband's assuming of a human form for some portion of the day or night) suggests that the heroine has only partly overcome her ambivalence about her relationship with her mate. While she may no longer regard him as threatening to herself (they can live compatibly together), apparently she still regards him as something unnatural or threatening in the context of her family. She must keep his animal disguise secret from them. The fact that his disappearance is linked to a problem in relating to her family suggests that the heroine is having trouble reconciling this new relationship and her attitude toward it with her preexisting social relationships and values. In other words, while the fact that her husband is frankly animalistic and sexually arousing is acceptable to the heroine, this does not mean that she is ready to have that aspect of her husband or of her attitude toward her husband be known around her family. The sexual role or persona of her mate is not one that the heroine can comfortably accept in the realm of her family.

The heroine's journey could also be regarded as an exploration of her unconscious mind whereby she is able to confront and overcome her latent fears. She must undertake a quest that symbolizes the problems she faces and the solutions to those problems. In "The Singing, Soaring Lark" the husband becomes a dove for seven years and leaves a red drop of blood and a white feather at every seventh step. In "The Iron Stove" the husband and his stove disappear. In both tales the heroine must undertake a long and arduous journey to another realm to reclaim her husband. The first story requires that she talk to various embodiments of nature, culminating in the night wind, while in the second the heroine gets assistance from a house full of toads. These figures and the mysterious world they inhabit may be understood as representing the heroine's unconscious mind. These fantastic figures symbolically represent her own feelings about herself and her world to some extent.

What she discovers in getting in touch with them is that, much like Dorothy in *The Wizard of Oz,* she possesses the inherent ability to overcome these problems and achieve her heart's desire. This is perhaps the most basic developmental lesson that is symbolically represented in fairy tales. The quintessential happy ending of these stories affirms this basic truth, that the protagonist and, accordingly, those who identify with her have the ability to surmount the obstacles that interfere with maturation and a successful transition to adulthood. In the case of this fairy tale, the obstacles concern primarily a false bride and an apparently powerless social and cosmic role. In both texts the protagonist is in competition with another bride, and in both tales the protagonist must overcome her subordinate and socially disenfranchised position in order to acquire her mate.

The initial part of the journey to an inner or supernatural realm confirms for the heroine her own value and powers. This confirmation is revealed in the fact that these representatives of the cosmic forces acknowledge her and help her and that, accordingly, she is able to accomplish her lengthy and arduous journeys and overcome the enchanted dragon, the glass mountain, the piercing swords, and the great lake. And the final part of her quest affirms for society in general and for those around her in particular, especially her mate, the heroine's worth. In other words, the first part of the journey is a personal exploration in which the heroine learns about herself and her relationship to cosmic forces and principles. She finds that she is more deserving and capable than she realized. The hidden resources that she acquires, the advice of the night wind and the magical reed, nut, casket, and egg in the first tale, and the help of the toads and the magical pins, plow-wheel, and the three nuts in the second, all point to qualities or abilities that she inherently has and simply discovers on this journey. They also point to a philosophical theme, for the prevalence of nuts and eggs suggests that procreation is an essential issue. By recognizing the procreative purpose of sexuality, the heroine, much like the heroine of "The

Goose-Girl," can learn to surmount her basic anxieties and moral prejudice against sexuality. She can learn to acknowledge the physical or animalistic aspect of her relationship to her husband, not only to herself, but also openly to her family and society, because sexuality serves the higher cosmic purpose of reproduction. Reminding herself of this truth, by opening the nut on the journey home in the first tale and by opening the egg in the second, enables the heroine to overcome her qualms about her relationship to her mate and to reclaim her husband in an open and socially sanctioned ceremony.

The key image in this concluding episode is the use of the magical dresses, which transform the heroine into not only something beautiful but also someone who is powerful and can manipulate others. Certainly, the very act of putting on a dress represents the successful socialization of the heroine; she is assimilating the cultural stereotype of what costume is appropriate for her gender. The dress marks her as a woman and indelibly separates her from men. The role afforded by this dress is shown to be reasonably effective; it can get the heroine what she wants, as long as what she wants corresponds to what society (through the fairy tale) wants her to want. In other words, the fine line between natural biological desires and socially fostered expectations is not always entirely clear in these fairy tales. In the end, the heroine's desires and her methods have become entirely socialized. The tale promotes total integration of personal, social, and cosmic values. Such a confluence is philosophically very functional and appealing, promoting a sense of wholeness and oneness with the world, but it is also philosophically naive and simplistic. Just as the moral caricature of the world is disingenuous in fairy tales, pretending the world can be neatly divided into good and evil, so this integrating of personal and cultural values into a scheme that is shown to be in harmony with the universe is somewhat optimistic and reductive. Individual wants cannot be so completely and exactly accommodated by social formulas: not every woman will become the queen of the castle, but traditional fairy tales gloss over the exceptions to and deviations from the social norm. They offer an appealing paradigm, a model that they suggest all can follow to some extent, but they do not recognize or treat the experiences of those who do not conform.

Thus, we find that there is a certain delimiting and basically sexist focus in female fairy tales, but this patriarchal social portrait is not the only or even the central emphasis of these tales. They also offer useful psychological metaphors of the personal anxieties audience members may be facing in coping with life's expectations and travails. In addition to socializing young female audience members into accepting the traditional roles and values of their culture, then, these stories also dramatize their reactions to those roles and conventions, offering them fictionalized reassurances that they can fulfill the demands placed on them. The texts do not question these demands; they accept as given what the society prescribes. Their job is to inform audiences of these expectations and try to help them to succeed. We must realize, however, that to inform without critcizing is to encourage conformity, and so these tales do serve a conservative function, sanctioning the patriarchal social structure.

The fairy tales with male protagonists also sanction the patriarchal system, for they too present an equally narrow portrait of what constitutes successful development. The adolescent males are supposed to find wives and establish kingdoms over which they will rule. While the biological urge for reproduction seems a reasonable goal, philosophically speaking the exclusive emphasis on this objective in the adolescent tales and the patriarchal form the marriage contract assumes in its implementation both call into question the universality and ultimate morality of such a message. Not every young man can expect to find a successful marriage partner, nor can he expect to be the ruler of the marriage. As a matter of fact, the latter expectation may well contribute to the difficulties in achieving the former.

In sum, while it is important to be aware of and acknowledge the sexist implications of the social formulas depicted in the symbolic realm of fairy tales, this recognition should not blind us to the more inclusive psychological insights also offered by the fairy tales. The stories are trying to show us metaphorically what we are, both socially and psychologically. Socially, they show us, if somewhat uncritically, just how phallocentric our society is. Psychologically, they show us the extent of our deepest fears and desires. Some critics seem to have difficulty accepting the flaws both in society and in human nature that these tales reveal. They tend to want to deny that these flaws are depicted in the tales, or else they want to blame the messenger for the bad news that it carries. We must be honest in our assessment of what these tales say and do for their audiences, and then we can continue to study them as invaluable cultural documents offering a record of the proclivities and prejudices of their audiences.

6

The Fairy Tale Influence in *The Wizard of Oz, The Cat in the Hat,* and *Where the Wild Things Are*

*T*he *Wizard of Oz, The Cat in the Hat,* and *Where the Wild Things Are* appeared over a sixty-year span in the twentieth century.[1] Each in its turn was arguably the most popular text of its time for the children's audiences that enjoy fairy tales. Their enormous popularity demonstrates the tremendous appeal of the fairy tale genre when it is adapted and used in literature. In each of these texts, the protagonists are ordinary young people with whom audiences tend to identify strongly. In each the protagonists encounter fantastic creatures who alternatively pose challenges for the protagonists or help them. As in traditional fairy tales, the fantastic creatures may be seen as exaggerated representations of the protagonists' fears and desires. Each text presents a quest or adventure in which, through their successful negotiation of the interaction with the magical or fantastic phenomena, the protagonists resolve their dilemmas or problems and return to a happy and harmonious family home with their parents. This interaction with the magical is presented earnestly and is suggested as a legitimate representation of the cosmos. In learning to recognize and accept this fantastic realm, the protagonists are both exploring and coming to terms with their unconscious selves, as well as acknowledging and communing with the supernatural dimension of the cosmos. As in the prepubescent subgenre of fairy tales, these texts present prepubescent protagonists whose ultimate goal is a successful reconciliation to their existing domestic situation, in other words, learning to get along with their parents by assimilating cultural norms and fulfilling social expectations.

While the formal elements of the plot and characterization of these texts closely resemble those of folk fairy tales, the style of narration does not. *The Wizard of Oz* is distinctly more of a children's novel, much longer and more elaborated with narrative details (such as the various colors that Baum assigns to the different regions of Oz) than the traditional fairy tale. *The Cat in the Hat* is a poem; the story is told in rhymed and metered verse. While traditional fairy tales do frequently include rhymes, they are never presented exclusively in poetic form. And *Where the Wild Things Are* is shorter than a traditional tale (it is only nine sentences long) and is told in an elliptical form that approaches poetry as well. Thus, in style all three texts show evidence of alternation that derives presumably from the different medium in which they are being presented. While the texts borrow freely from the fairy tale genre in matters of the plot, characters, and themes (as we shall presently document), in the matter of style—the choice of sentence structure, syntax, diction, dialogue, and the use of poetic devices—these texts depart from the traditional forms and formulas of fairy tales and incorporate stylistic options popular in other literary texts.

The Wizard of Oz

Like many traditional fairy tales, *The Wizard of Oz* begins with a problematic domestic situation. In the tradition of many fairy tale heroines (such as Cinderella, Snow White, and the heroine in "The Kind and Unkind Girls"), Dorothy feels unloved and unappreciated at home and does not get along well with her mother, or the woman serving in the role of the mother. As is frequently the case in other fairy tales, the mother's role in *The Wizard of Oz* is filled by a substitute, a surrogate mother, who performs the duties of the mother without the love and care the child yearns for. In chapter 1, Aunt Em is described as follows: "She was thin and gaunt, and never smiled now. When Dorothy, who was an orphan, first came to her, Aunt Em had been so startled by the child's laughter that she would scream and press her hand upon her heart whenever Dorothy's merry voice reached her ears; and she still looked at the little girl with wonder that she could find anything to laugh at" (10). This picture of a stern, even hostile, mother figure corresponds to the mother roles in the fairy tales listed above, and like many of these fairy tales, the heroine's real mother is missing. Thus, in addition to the mother's role being drawn from fairy tales, the role of Dorothy as a poor little waif at the mercy of an unpleasant mother figure is also borrowed from traditional fairy tales. Dorothy's role as an orphan duplicates in effect the role of Cinderella, Snow White, and a host of other fairy tale stepdaughters.

The essence of this characterization in fairy tales of a conflict between an oppressive mother figure and a powerless and pitiable young heroine is a representation of a typical domestic crisis experienced by young girls. In other words, these stories base their appeal on tapping into the emotions of audience members who have felt some conflict or hostility toward their mothers. The fairy tales exaggerate and dramatize this underlying psychological conflict by having the natural mother be replaced by an unrealistically hostile mother figure. Snow White's mother is replaced in the Grimms' version by a wicked queen who wants to kill the heroine. Similarly, the stepmother in "Cinderella" treats her stepdaughter like a servant or slave. In *The Wizard of Oz*, not only is Auntie Em presented as a cold substitute for a mother, but when Dorothy enters the world of Oz she encounters even more overtly hostile mother figures, the Wicked Witches of the East and West. Baum borrows the fairy tale device of polarizing the child's attitude toward her mother; however, he doubles the fairy tale's polarization by presenting four witches: two supremely good and two unmitigatedly evil. These polarized portraits represent the young girl's ambivalence toward her mother: loving and supportive on the one hand (like the good witch who gives Dorothy the kiss on her forehead), and yet demanding and antagonistic on the other (like the wicked witch who wants to steal the shoes that rightfully belong to Dorothy). The shoes represent the role, the social position that the young girl wants to fulfill and that society expects her to assume. In the young girl's mind, her mother is to some degree an obstacle to attaining that role, in part because the child naively thinks that in order to assume that role she must displace her mother completely. She feels that her maturation to some extent involves competition with the mother.

Baum also borrows the fairy tale technique of having his heroine journey into a magical realm that serves as a fantasized representation of her unconscious mind. This is illustrated in part by having exaggeratedly good and evil mother figures dominate this realm. They represent the two unconscious attitudes the heroine has toward her mother. In addition, the presence of color in the world of Oz, in contrast to its absence in Kansas, reflects the emotional warmth, vitality, and energy of her unconscious mind, which is contrasted with the already documented emotional stasis and barrenness of her conscious and quotidian existence. In journeying into this realm, she is getting in touch with her feelings, which have been repressed at home (her conscious day-to-day existence) as a result of her emotional conflict with and alienation from her mother. (In the film version, Dorothy's adventures in Oz are ultimately represented as a dream she has, much like *Alice's Adventures in Wonderland*. While this representation does, on the one hand, help confirm the unconscious nature of the content of the adventures, on the other hand, it detracts from the epistemological validity of the fantasy. The events may be dismissed as the illogical associations of a dreaming mind, rather than regarded as evidence of some deeper or higher truths, or of a more accurate and essential way of viewing the world.)

Other evidence in support of reading Oz as a figurative representation of the heroine's unconscious mind include the companions she meets there and the tasks she must complete. Her companions represent aspects of herself—her low intellectual self-esteem (the scarecrow, who literally feels as if he were born yesterday), her emotional repression and frigidity (the tin man, who is protected and encumbered by his suit of armor, which was a result of an unhappy romance, and who fears accordingly that he cannot feel anything), and her lack of moral assurance (the cowardly lion, who lacks the courage of his own convictions). That each of these companions possesses the very qualities that he so dearly wants and feels he does not have reveals that the heroine has these qualities already inside herself; it is just a matter of recognizing and utilizing these abilities she inherently possesses. This message is of considerable reassurance to children in the process of maturation.

As far as the heroine's tasks go, she must find her way home, but only after destroying the Wicked Witch of the West, exposing the sham of the Wizard of Oz, and finding Glinda, the Good Witch of the South. The first and foremost task of destroying the wicked witch represents the elimination of the child's negative perception of her mother. That the Wicked Witch of the West represents a hostile mother figure is confirmed by how she treats Dorothy once she captures her. She makes Dorothy do household chores, just like any other mother. She also puts invisible iron bars in Dorothy's way, interfering with her ability to perform her tasks and fulfill her role as a member of the household. These invisible iron bars are an appropriate metaphor of the child's feeling that her mother has a hostile attitude toward her and wants to prevent her successful maturation.

The way Dorothy eliminates the wicked witch, by throwing a bucket of water on her, reveals that the witch is only an illusion, an insubstantial image subject to dissolution when brought into contact with something as true and pure as water. Baum's choice of having his heroine actively eliminate her antagonist is watered down, if you will, in the film version, where Dorothy accidentally gets the witch wet in trying to put out the fire on the scarecrow's straw. The difference is illuminating. Baum's heroine is allowed to get angry and act decisively on her feelings, a positive and nonsexist representation. She uses the bucket of water as a weapon, much as the male protagonists of other fairy tales use their swords; it is a gender-appropriate and effective means of dispatching her adversary and affirming the propriety of her moral position.

The little girl, seeing that she had lost one of her pretty shoes, grew angry, and said to the Witch, "Give me back my shoe!"

"I will not," retorted the Witch, "for it is now my shoe and not yours."

"You are a wicked creature!" cried Dorothy. "You have no right to take my shoe from me."

"I shall keep it, just the same," said the Witch, laughing at her, "and someday I shall get the other one from you, too."

This made Dorothy so very angry that she picked up the bucket of water that stood near and dashed it over the Witch, wetting her from head to foot.

Instantly the wicked woman gave a loud cry of fear, and then, as Dorothy looked at her in wonder, the Witch began to shrink and fall away. (105–6)

In contrast, the cinematographic Dorothy can only act in consonance with sexist and patriarchal notions that women are fundamentally not hostile and aggressive. She acts only out of sympathy and compassion for the plight of the scarecrow, not out of anger and righteous indignation for her own plight. Thus, the movie version deprives audiences of the model of a female protagonist acting decisively and authoritatively to uphold and secure her moral place in the world. Baum's text is representative of and appeals to a somewhat more liberated and egalitarian audience that is ready to see heroines dispatch their adversaries personally and actively.

The point of the heroine's journey is specifically to kill, to eliminate, the wicked witch. This goal is implicitly revealed when we see that the initial crossing of the threshold between the two realms results in the killing of one of the wicked witches. This shows that the heroine is on the right course, and that course involves the destruction of the evil witches. In effect, one half of the problem is eliminated simply by undertaking the journey, in other words, by beginning to get in touch with her feelings. That the Wicked Witch of the East rules the munchkins (a play on the German term for a little child) reveals her role as a repressive mother figure, dominating Dorothy's unconscious mind. Thus, the wicked witches together symbolize Dorothy's negative attitude toward a mother, and the purpose of her journey is to resolve these hostile feelings. By admitting the problem and seeking to get in touch with her deepest feelings (by letting herself be carried away by the cyclone, a metaphor of the violent emotions swirling inside of her), Dorothy has begun the crucial and therapeutic process of self-exploration.

What she finds in her unconscious realm is that it is ruled excessively by these authoritarian mother figures, and her task is to bring some balance, some order to this world. She must work to assert the power of the good witches and diminish the power of the wicked ones. In effect, this is the advice of the Wizard of Oz, who serves in the role of a father figure to whom the girl goes for advice. While his advice is appropriate, the story shows the heroine that she cannot rely completely on this figure. He is a sham, an illusion. The interesting point is that he realizes that he is a fake and that it is the little people of Oz, again much like the munchkins, who represent the childish aspect of Dorothy and who have made him into the charlatan that he is. In other words, the idealizing and idolizing of the father by the child results in the child's looking up to the father as a great figure, all out of proportion to what he is in real life. Dorothy must learn to see through or past the illusions to the real person who was her father, just as she must learn to see and appreciate her real mother. She must de-idealize the father of her fantasy.

After exposing the charade of the Wizard, Dorothy wrongly concludes: "I think you are a very bad man." The Wizard replies, "Oh no, my dear; I'm really a very good man; but I'm a very bad wizard, I must admit" (129). Ironically, it was Dorothy (in the guise of the inhabitants of Oz, her own unconscious mind) who had believed that the man in the balloon, who was apparently a powerful figure on high, was a wizard. This naive conceptualization is a result of an immature and inappropriate epistemological assessment of the person. This faulty outlook is metaphorically depicted in the text by the circumstance that everyone in Oz wears glasses with green lenses. Like children, they do not see the world correctly and realistically, but through the bias of their own assumptions, which Dorothy must learn to leave behind.

She does, thanks to the help of the dog Toto, her instinctive and animalistic side, which impulsively rushes in to confront problems and wrestles with the various dilemmas that Dorothy confronts. The function of Toto is once more to confirm to audience members that Dorothy and they carry within themselves the natural ability to surmount the problems they face. Toto is an affirmation of the instinctive force that keeps us going and helps us achieve our goals. From the beginning, it is Toto who makes Dorothy laugh, revealing his direct connection to her true feelings and emotions. Furthermore, it is Toto who pulls back the curtain, revealing the charade of the Wizard. Appropriately, in the end, it is Toto who does not let Dorothy return home with the Wizard in the balloon. Toto decides to chase a cat—to follow his own instincts. He works to prevent Dorothy from relying on her father to get her through her problems, because she must work them out for herself and find her own way home. He represents Dorothy's primitive, instinctual self, which serves the useful function of focusing directly and relentlessly on its goal, but which must work in harmony with the rational mind to achieve success.

Dorothy's last task is to journey to Glinda, the Good Witch of the South, thereby effecting a reconciliation with the positive side of the mother. Through identification with the good image of the mother, the child learns what it is to be a woman. This character can serve as a model for her, as well as a friend and confidante. Accordingly, it is Glinda who tells her that she possessed the ability to get back home all along. By her words and her example, she shows Dorothy how to fill her role as a woman. She also reassures the child, once again, that she inherently possesses all the qualities necessary to fulfill the role. She already has the Silver Shoes, the symbol of her place in society that she is in the process of filling. She need only recognize that she has achieved her goal.

Her desire "to get back to Kansas" (166) is not a retrogressive impulse to return to things as they once were. While in part it might represent separation anxiety and childish insecurities about being on one's own, it also represents a desire to be at home, to be in loving contact with her Auntie Em. Only by working through the fears and resentments dramatically and fantastically portrayed in the story can the heroine achieve this goal of being at one with her mother. The plot and the motifs of the story follow the fairy tale model, dramatically depicting the maturation of its protagonist in graphic and imaginative ways. While there is no doubt that, as some historians have pointed out, Baum's story functions in part as a populist allegory (revealing the falseness of the gold standard and the benefits of the silver standard, a major political issue of the turn of the century), this theme does not by any means account for the central appeal of the tale. It is still popular in spite of its outdated sociopolitical message. Audiences who continue to enjoy this story do so, not because they have some latent interest in nineteenth-century economic upheavals, but because they have a subliminal empathy with a heroine who faces the challenges of overcoming her own insecurities and anxieties and because they enjoy the fairy tale–like depiction of the overcoming of those challenges.

The Cat in the Hat

The Cat in the Hat also dramatically depicts the psychological struggles of its young protagonist through fantastic imagery that follows the fairy tale model. It begins with two children sitting alone and bored in their house. Their boredom almost reduces them to a catatonic state, staring blankly out the window, when a cat walks in through their front door. Like the intrusion of other fantastic characters in various fairy tales ("The Cat as Helper," AT 545), this disruption may be seen as the externalization of the unconscious concerns of the audience members, who identify with the plight of the protagonist. In other words, the cat represents the children's mischievous impulse, which yearns to violate the rules and norms of the household in order to gain some pleasure, some fun.

As Campbell puts it, the cat (like the cyclone in *The Wizard of Oz*) serves as a call to adventure, a signal that not everything is satisfactory in the present situation and that the protagonists must set about doing something to resolve the underlying problems. The cat and the cyclone represent both the main problem in their respective stories as well as the means of resolving that problem. In *The Wizard of Oz* the cyclone represents the violent emotions that lurk beneath the surface of the heroine's psyche and that she must work out, and it also represents the means for resolving those emotions, by carrying Dorothy across the threshold of her conscious mind into the world of her unconscious. In *The Cat in the Hat*, the appearance of the cat is a recognition of and a response to the stagnating and suffocating influence of social conformity. The children's boredom essentially puts the children to sleep (sends them into their unconscious mind) where they encounter the fantasized image of their own playful impulses, which yearn to be released. Release them they do, as the children let first the cat and then Thing One and Thing Two run free in the house.

The problem metaphorically depicted in the fantastic imagery of *The Cat in the Hat* extends beyond mere boredom, however. The story is about balancing and reconciling contradictory impulses in the child's own psyche. While the cat represents the playful side, another fantastic character emerges in opposition to the cat. The little goldfish says, "Make that cat go away, he should not be here when your mother is not." The goldfish is the voice of the child's conditioned conscience. He attempts to discipline the cat, but as their relative fantasized images suggest, the mischievous side has the upper hand at this point.

Dr. Seuss has ingeniously selected two absolutely appropriate metaphoric figures to represent these contradictory impulses in the child. On the one hand, the cat reminds us of the animalistic side of the child. Cats are mysterious creatures who roam the night and largely follow their own impulses; they correspond to the instinctive side of the child. Furthermore, they are superstitiously associated with witches, magic, and the supernatural world. This wild behavior is not recognized initially as being of their own doing or volition; the spirit or force intrudes from outside. This rationalization is similarly depicted in fairy tales, such as "My Mother Slew Me; My Father Ate Me/The Juniper Tree" (AT 720), that offer the Christian rationalization that the devil made the person behave badly. Evil is projected outward on some cosmic explanation, which exonerates to some degree the actions of the culpable individuals.

As the awareness of the protagonist develops, however, this exculpatory representation gives way to the realization that the mischievousness is part of the children themselves. This is reflected in the emergence of Thing One and Thing Two. Once again they come from the mysterious outside domain, and they are brought by the cat, so they extend and underscore the same symbolic associations with supernatural cosmic agency. Moreover, they are kept locked in a box, suggesting their wildness and dangerousness. The locked box may also be read as a metaphor of the mechanism of repression operating in their unconscious to keep these wild urges from surfacing and running amok. By letting Thing One and Thing Two out of the box, the children are releasing their own primitive instincts and impulses, as revealed by the wild, childish games these creatures engage in.

These two new metaphoric representations illustrate, moreover, the evolution of the children's awareness of this wild energy. The first thing they do is to shake hands with these new creatures ("And Sally and I / Did not know what to do / So we had to shake hands / With Thing One and Thing Two"), revealing that the children are recognizing these impulses and beginning to accept them as having some significant relation to themselves. Even as they acknowledge these impulses, they fall back on formal social conventions. The fact that there are now two metaphoric figures, just as there are two children, that these figures are diminutive, just like the children, and that they are human shaped, unlike the cat, suggests a growing awareness that the primitive impulse the cat embodies is not entirely a foreign and external force for the children, but is rather something very much like them and very likely a part of them.

In opposition to these denizens of the dark and anarchic realm, these agents of the wild and playful spirit lurking both in the cosmos and in the children, the story presents the character of the goldfish. He is the voice of conventional morality, the advocate of the mother's values and code of behavior. He tells the cat to leave and chides him when his games result in the destruction of the household. The fantastic figure of the fish is an appropriate metaphor of this moral impulse in the children. The fish lives in the confined and socialized world of the goldfish bowl. He lives an ordered and predictable existence, swimming back and forth within the boundaries of this world. He also exists beneath the surface of the water, just as the conscience exists in the children's unconscious mind. Furthermore, he is cold-blooded, which is in direct opposition to the hot-blooded and impulsive nature of the cat. This cold-bloodedness is suggestive of the rationality that underlies morality. It is the rational awareness of consequences that leads in turn to acceptance of the reality principle, which is the essence of morality, the realization of the consequences of one's behavior that requires one to modify one's behavior. The fish is aware of possible consequences; he worries about the damage that the wild behavior will cause, because he is rational, unlike the cat, who is controlled exclusively by the pleasure principle. The fact that cats and fish are natural enemies reinforces further this metaphoric opposition operating in the text and reveals the relative appeal and corresponding influence of these two principles for the children. The lure of the emotional self-gratification embodied in the cat is stronger at this point than the inclination to follow the moral guidelines and conform to the socialized ethics represented by the fish.

The embodiments of the children's instinctive emotions, Thing One and Thing Two, violate the basic rules of the house, playing outdoor games inside and leading the children to invade the sanctum of the mother's bedroom (the father is not mentioned, nor is there any evidence of him in the bedroom). In exploring this bedroom, these creatures are externalizing not only the children's playful and mischievous nature, but also their basic instinct of curiosity. Accordingly, the kite of Thing One pulls out of the closet (another metaphor of the unconscious and its store of repressed images and feelings) a dress with red and pink polka dots, while the kite of Thing Two bumps the head of the mother's bed. That the dress and bed are so emphasized corresponds to the cartoonlike characteristic of fairy tales to focus on salient images and to exclude unnecessary detail.

The dress and the bed represent two issues about which these developing children have considerable curiosity and no little concern—gender identity and sexual procreativity. The dress is for them what marks women as different from men. Appropriately, the red-and-white color contrast of the dress is reminiscent of the red-and-white apple in the Grimm's version of "Snow White." Both stories are, in part, epistemological narratives; that is, they depict the intellectual development of the protagonists as they move from innocence (the purity of the whiteness and the corresponding ignorance of gender difference and the role of sexuality) to experience (the redness representing awareness of the vital truths of life, the blood of life so to speak). The other details emphasized in the illustration are also items illustrating the mother's femininity—her perfume, brush, and mirror. Similarly, having the kite bump into the head of the bed represents the child's metaphorically coming into contact with the ideas symbolically associated with the bed, in particular the mystery of adult sexuality and the taboo of oedipal desire.

Thus, the embodiments of the child's instinctive and curious impulses, Thing One and Thing Two (themselves so primitive and abstract that they have only generic names), lead the children (and especially the first-person narrator) to explore and confront subliminal feelings, both in terms of behavior (acting rebelliously and indulging curiosity) as well as in terms of subject matter (confronting repressed preoccupations about what goes on in the parent's bedroom, what is the difference between male and female, and what is the nature of one's feelings about one's parent of the opposite sex).

Soon after this climactic experience, the narrator decides that he does not like the way that Thing One and Thing Two play. This decision may be seen either as an indication that he regards his instinctive and impulsive side as having fulfilled its usefulness or that he regards his wild impulse as having overstepped the bounds of propriety so far as to have made him psychologically uncomfortable. In any case, once he decides he does not like the way they make him act, the metaphoric representation of his conscience changes from the ineffectual and tiny fish to the imposing and authoritarian image of the mother. The mother herself does not reappear initially; it is only the threat of her impending return, a reassertion of the moral values that the child has absorbed from her, that now once more guides the children's behavior. By identifying with the mother's morality and criticizing the behavior of the wild things, the child effects a metamorphosis in his attitude toward the importance and power of his conscience, which is reflected in the replacement of the easily ignored fish with the intimidating icon of the mother. (A similar metaphoric metamorphosis takes place in another equally popular literary fairy tale, *Pinocchio,* when the tiny and ineffectual cricket is replaced by the Blue Fairy.)[2]

Thus, the appeal and significance of *The Cat in the Hat* for millions of children can be traced quite directly to its fairy tale–like representation of a basic morality conflict experienced by all children. It uses ordinary protagonists who encounter exaggerated fantasized images that symbolize fundamental developmental issues of concern to audience members. And the story ends happily, with the feelings confronted and reconciled.

Part of the philosophical value of this text is that is does not simplistically and puritanically dismiss the cat and the instinctive, animalistic impulse that he represents. While the story shows that these impulses are antisocial and dangerous if allowed free rein—they destroy the house and lure the children into confronting feelings that they may not be ready for—the story also shows that this emotional and impulsive side has a constructive function as well. Of its own volition, the cat returns to help clean up the house. The cat is amoral, not immoral. Its primitive energies can be directed to good, useful, and nonselfish activities, and when they are, it seems as if the work gets done of its own accord (the cat rides a machine with many hands that pick up the mess in a flash). In other words, one can and should harness the instinctive impulses for constructive accomplishments.

Thus, the story may be seen as offering a psychological allegory, depicting the battle between two parts of the mind—the instincts versus the conscience. Ultimately, this conflict is resolved by the balancing agent in the mind, the child's own sense of self-identity, which is who he thinks he really is and which determines what he really wants to listen to. Like traditional fairy tales, *The Cat in the Hat* offers a very basic primer in self-awareness expressed in the metaphoric and exaggerated language of fantasy. It focuses on an ordinary protagonist who wrestles with typical developmental concerns of interest to most individuals who would identify chronologically and emotionally with the protagonist. These concerns are fundamentally personal and psychological in nature. They involve social and cosmic issues as well, but these are presented primarily from the point of view of the individual psyche. Conforming to social expectations, for example, is seen as a matter of listening to one's own conscience or not. The fairy tale, both traditional and literary, is, by its formal characteristic, inherently preoccupied with the mental landscape of the protagonist, intrinsically directed at depicting and coming to terms with the latent anxieties, emotions, desires, and urges of its protagonist and, by extension, its audience members. *The Cat in the Hat* uses the fantastic plot, symbolism, and themes characteristic of fairy tales to perform much the same function as traditional fairy tales—to provide its audience members with a fictionalized means of confronting their most basic concerns. This text teaches children to assimilate their instinctual, fun, mischievous side, in a healthy and controlled way, rather than engaging in the extremes of completely sup-pressing or giving in to these impulses. It teaches children how to balance their psyches, such that they will no longer be bored by exaggerated, simplistic conformity to moral prescriptions, nor will they run wild in the house, but rather use their imaginations to entertain themselves in playful, fantastic, and socially accept-able ways.

Where the Wild Things Are

Another very popular literary fairy tale that exemplifies this psy-chological focus is Maurice Sendak's *Where the Wild Things Are*, which recounts the fantastic experiences of a little boy named Max. The story uses the fundamental plot of many fairy tales, the journey to a magical land of a young and sympathetic hero, much like that in "Jack and the Beanstalk," to portray the moral development of its protagonist. While this story alters the tradi-tional characterization of its protagonist somewhat—he is not presented initially as morally pure—he is nonetheless a young and appealing character. Furthermore, his moral imperfections are eventually corrected through the symbolic lessons offered in the fantastic adventure, according to the fairy tale formula. The fantastic characters are taken seriously by the story, and they serve to reveal certain philosophical and psychological truths of importance to the protagonist.

Max behaves somewhat roughly at the beginning of the story, pounding nails in his mother's walls to set up a make-believe tent and chasing the dog with a fork. His mother calls him a "wild thing," and when he retaliates by threatening to eat her up, she sends him to bed without his dinner. Thus, this story begins with a domestic problem—just like a host of fairy tales. However, this story is different. Typically in fairy tales, the pro-tagonist is depicted as innocent, or at least naive, as not bearing any responsibility for the problem that surfaces. For example, the lack of food and ensuing domestic crisis in "Jack and the Beanstalk" is a product of Jack's foolishness or simplicity in believing that the beans are magical and will be of some use to them (it turns out, of course, that they are and they do). Jack's mother is disappointed in her son and his foolishness in trading their cow for beans, but it is clear that Jack's impulse is essentially moral and benign, if somewhat impractical or silly. Most fairy tales about young protagonists are equally unequivocal about their protagonist's moral purity; it is their inherent goodness (which is a product both of how young audience members would naively want to see themselves and of how society wants them to see themselves) that enables them to succeed in the end.

In contrast, Max in *Where the Wild Things Are* acts out of rebelliousness and impishness, qualities that fairy tale protagonists do not traditionally manifest. In Max's case, the problem is somewhat more honestly and realistically connected to the protagonist. Deviating from fairy tales such as "Three Hairs from the Devil's Beard," in which the protagonist is portrayed as an entirely innocent victim of the domestic hostility he encounters, Sendak portrays Max as overtly acting out his mischievous impulses, much to the dismay and disapproval of his mother. The audience can sense that Max's hanging of his teddy bear and threatening of the dog with a fork are examples of inappropriate behavior. They are childish, but potentially dangerous, actions that deserve to be chastised. The problem is not only that Max is doing these things, but that he does not understand why his mother thinks they are wrong. From his point of view, he is only having fun and has no intention of actually hurting anybody, much like the Cat in the Hat. The point is that our behavior must take into account the point of view of others, but Max has not yet learned this important moral lesson. The exaggerated and fantastic imagery of the journey teaches him, and audience members who identify with him, this lesson.

The journey begins when Max's room turns into a jungle, a boat sails by, and Max gets in it. It takes him to where the wild things are. Sendak has masterfully done what fairy tales traditionally do; he presents an exaggerated externalized image of the protagonist's inner conflict. In this case, the conflict is with his own wild or mischievous self. It has gotten him into trouble and he cannot understand why. Thus, he journeys to explore these feelings. The sea journey that lasts over a year is a traditional metaphor of the crossing into the realm of the unconscious (what Campbell calls the threshold crossing).

The connection between Max and these wild things is quite apparent as a result of Sendak's visual rendering of narrative moments. First of all, when he was engaged in his mischief, Max was dressed in a wild-animal suit that greatly resembles the appearance of the wild things. Second, the wild things ultimately threaten to eat him up, just as he threatened his mother. Third, after his confrontation with them, he sends them to bed without supper, just as his mother did to him. Finally, the wild things behave in a mischievous and apparently threatening manner just as he did, and they all participate in the wild rumpus together as the climax of Max's adventure in the fantasy realm. These connections all confirm that the wild things represent Max's wild side, and his adventure involves a coming to terms with these impulses.

What he discovers is the golden rule: do unto others as you would have them do unto you. When he confronts the wild things, he is now on the receiving end of the impish and playful behavior; the shoe is on the other foot, as it were. He finds that it does not feel pleasant when they "roared their terrible roars and gnashed their terrible teeth and rolled their terrible eyes and showed their terrible claws." He begins to realize that it is not as much fun being the potential victim of such threatening behavior as it is to be the dispenser. Max has the courage of his convictions, however; he stares into their yellow eyes without blinking once. That is to say, he is able to confront and acknowledge his own wild impulses and to subordinate them to his moral conscience. They make him king of all the wild things, and he orders that the rumpus begin. The rumpus teaches audience members that the wild side may be enjoyed as long as it is done within certain guidelines and under certain restrictions. As long as everyone is playing the same game, and the game takes place in the proper venue (outside preferably), then the mischievous behavior is acceptable, perhaps even necessary, given the existence of this wild nature in all of us.

Where the Wild Things Are teaches a valuable moral lesson about acknowledging and coming to terms with one's emotional and instinctive impulses. By confronting his own wildness and acting out the role of the mother, Max learns the rationale for his mother's moral judgment of him and incorporates her morality into himself. He learns not only the reason for the moral censure, but also the means of implementing that ethical code. Once the lesson is learned, however, there is no need to linger in the solipsistic realm of his own unconscious. He becomes lonely and yearns to return. Much like Dorothy in *The Wizard of Oz*, the protagonist comes to a new understanding of a parent figure, which then allows him to appreciate and to want to be with that parent figure again. Max sails back for weeks until he returns to his own room, where he finds his supper waiting for him, still hot.

While there are certain variations in the fairy tale form that this story assumes, namely the elliptical narration, the poetic syntax, and the initially realistic characterization of the protagonist, overall, *Where the Wild Things Are* makes excellent use of the essential qualities of the genre. It presents a sympathetic youthful protagonist who embarks on an adventurous quest that entails an exploration of a fantastic realm. This realm is presented earnestly; Sendak in no way suggests that this realm is any less believable or significant than the primary world inhabited by Max's mother. And the fantastic encounter teaches the protagonist a very valuable lesson—the importance of controlling one's wild urges. Finally, the story ends happily, with Max once more in the comfort and security of his family. The still-hot dinner suggests that Max is loved by his mother, who will continue to nurture and protect him. It also suggests that Max has been reincorporated back into the social clan of the family structure. His rebellious independence has been curbed. The food is both a token of the clan's acceptance of him and a sign of his acceptance of them and their morality.

Thus, this story, like the previous two literary fairy tales of *The Wizard of Oz* and *The Cat in the Hat*, follows the fairy tale model by employing the essential characteristics of that genre. They all incorporate magic or fantasy in such a manner that its epistemological and ontological validity is affirmed; they all incorporate an adventure or quest, which entails the interaction with an unknown, magical, and mysterious realm; they all present the successful completion of that quest in such a way that the moral propriety of the universe is affirmed; they all present an ordinary and youthful protagonist with whom we identify unambiguously; and finally, they all depict themes of basic interest to audiences about the typical concerns of their lives, primarily developmental issues about maturation.

These literary fairy tales serve to illustrate the underlying form and function of the genre as a whole. Whether these narratives circulate in oral tradition or in a literary text, they share a common purpose as well as a common artistic heritage. They attempt to speak to the soul, the *psyche*, of their audiences, and, accordingly, they use an exaggerated and fantastic language in order to communicate with this hidden part of ourselves. They follow a formula that reveals to us the possibility of self-discovery. This knowledge about the self is shown to be the key to social integration and cosmic harmony. Thus, the happy ending of fairy tales is an affirmation of what we can know and can accomplish. It is a celebration of what we can become if we listen to the magical voices inside our heads. The form of the fairy tale carries with it an epistemological and philosophical statement about how we can know the world and ourselves, and how this knowledge can help us to lead successful lives. On the whole, it is not an unimportant lesson that is offered in these unpretentious, perennially popular tales.

Notes

CHAPTER 1

1. Jacob and Wilhelm Grimm, *The Complete Grimm's Fairy Tales,* trans. Margaret Hunt, rev. James Stern (New York: Pantheon Books, 1972), 249–58. See also A. S. Macquisten and R. W. Pickford, "Psychological Aspects of the Fantasy of Snow White and the Seven Dwarfs," *Psychoanalytic Review* 29 (1942), 233–52, which discusses the history of the collection of that folktale; Steven Swann Jones, *The New Comparative Method: Structural and Symbolic Analysis of the Allomotifs of "Snow White,"* FF Communications No. 247 (Helsinki: Academia Scientiarum Fennica, 1990), 10–12; and Heinz Rölleke, "The 'Utterly Hessian' Fairy Tales by 'Old Marie': The End of a Myth," in *Fairy Tales and Society: Illusion, Allusion, and Paradigm,* ed. Ruth B. Bottigheimer (Philadelphia: University of Pennsylvania Press, 1986), 287–300.

2. Giovanni Batiste Basile, *Il Pentamerone: or, The Tale of Tales,* trans. Sir Richard Burton (New York: Liveright, 1943).

3. Bengt Holbek, *Interpretation of Fairy Tales: Danish Folklore in a European Perspective,* FF Communications No. 239 (Helsinki: Academia Scientiarum Fennica, 1987).

4. Johannes Bolte and George Polívka, *Anmerkungen zu den Kinder- und Hausmarchen der Brüder Grimm*, 5 vols. (Leipzig: Dieterichsche Verlagsbuchhandlung, 1913–32).

5. Antti Aarne, *Verzeichnis der Marchentypen*, FF Communications No. 3 (Helsinki: Academia Scientiarum Fennica, 1912).

6. Antti Aarne and Stith Thompson, *The Types of the Folktale: A Classification and Bibliography*, FF Communications No. 184 (Helsinki: Academia Scientiarum Fennica, 1973).

7. Hans Christian Andersen, *Eighty Fairy Tales* (New York: Pantheon Books, 1976).

8. Stith Thompson, *The Folktale* (Berkeley: University of California Press, 1977).

9. Axel Olrik, "The Epic Laws of Folk Narrative," in *The Study of Folklore*, ed. Alan Dundes (Englewood Cliffs, N.J.: Prentice-Hall, 1965), 129–41; Max Lüthi, *Once Upon a Time: On the Nature of Fairy Tales*, trans. Lee Chadeayne and Paul Gottwald (Bloomington: Indiana University Press, 1976); and Bruno Bettelheim, *The Uses of Enchantment: The Meaning and Importance of Fairy Tales* (New York: Random House, Vintage Books, 1977).

10. See Sigmund Freud, *Interpretation of Dreams*, trans. James Strachey (New York: Avon Books, 1965), as well as *The Occurrence in Dreams of Material from Fairy Tales* (London: Hogarth Press, 1913), and his coauthored study with D. E. Oppenheim, "Dreams in Folklore," in the *Standard Edition of the Complete Psychological Works of Sigmund Freud*, trans. James Strachey, ed. Anna Freud et al. (London: Hogarth, 1959), vol. 12, 177–211; Carl Jung, *Symbols of Transformation* and *The Archetypes and the Collective Unconscious*, vol. 5 and vol. 9, respectively, of *The Collected Works of C. G. Jung*, ed. William McGuire (Princeton: Princeton University Press, 1970); Géza Róheim, *The Gates of the Dream* (New York: International Universities Press, 1952) and "Dame Holle: Dream and Folktale" in *Explorations in Psychoanalysis*, ed. Robert Lindner (New York: Julian Press, 1953), 84–94; Max Lüthi, *The European Folktale: Form and Nature*, trans. John D. Niles (Bloomington: Indiana University Press, 1982), *Once Upon a Time: On the Nature of Fairy Tales*, and *The Fairy Tale*

as Art Form and Portrait of Man, trans. Jon Erickson (Bloomington: Indiana University Press, 1984); Erich Fromm, *The Forgotten Language: An Introduction to the Understanding of Dreams, Fairy Tales and Myths* (New York: Rinehart, 1951); Joseph Campbell, *The Hero with a Thousand Faces* (Princeton: Princeton University Press, 1970); and Bettelheim, *The Uses of Enchantment.*

11. Max Lüthi, *The European Folktale; Once Upon a Time: On the Nature of Fairy Tales;* and *The Fairy Tale as Art Form and Portrait of Man.*

12. Antoine de Saint-Exupéry, *The Little Prince,* trans. Katherine Woods (New York: Reynal & Hitchcock, 1943).

13. See Lüthi, *The European Folktale;* Campbell, *The Hero with a Thousand Faces;* Bettelheim, *The Uses of Enchantment;* and Vladimir Propp, *Morphology of the Folktale* (Austin: University of Texas Press, 1968).

14. Vladimir Propp, *Theory and History of Folklore* (Minneapolis: University of Minnesota Press, 1984).

15. Arnold van Gennep, *The Rites of Passage* (Chicago: University of Chicago Press, 1960); Carl Jung, *Symbols of Transformation,* vol. 5 of *The Collected Works of C. G. Jung,* ed. William McGuire (Princeton: Princeton University Press, 1970); Victor Turner, *The Ritual Process: Structure and Anti-Structure* (Ithaca, N.Y.: Cornell University Press, 1977).

CHAPTER 2

1. The concept of "adult" fairy tales with adult protagonists is presented in two excellent studies by Allan B. Chinen. In *In the Ever After: Fairy Tales and the Second Half of Life* (Wilmette, Ill.: Chiron Publications, 1989), Chinen discusses tales for old people or elders, which, according to Chinen, constitute approximately 5 percent of the entire corpus of fairy tales. In *Once Upon a Midlife: Classical Stories and Mythic Tales to Illuminate the Middle Years* (Los Angeles: Jeremy P. Tarcher, 1992), he retells tales with middle-aged protagonists, which constitute about 10 percent of the fairy tale corpus, in order to show how they illustrate the problems and challenges of the middle years. Thus, Chinen concurs with my findings

that in addition to the majority of children's fairy tales (which constitute about 85 percent of the fairy tale corpus and which I divide into pre- and postpubescent narratives), there are a significant number of adult tales (which he divides into middle and elder tales). Chinen's studies also share with this study a number of important precepts. He points out that fairy tales "emphasize universal themes" (*Once Upon,* 7) and that comparison of multiple texts is crucial for accurate intepretation (*Once Upon,* 6). Chinen also observes that these tales are essentially symbolic narratives that offer "a clear conduit to the unconscious" because they use an alternative "mode of thought" (*Once Upon,* 2). Along this line, Chinen cites Jerome Bruner's labeling of the distinction between the rational, logical mode versus the imaginative, symbolic mode as the difference between the *scientific* and the *narrative* (what I refer to as the logical versus the analogical). He cites, as well, Gisela Labouvie-Vief's labeling of these two modes as *logos* and *mythos*. According to Chinen, "By any name, stories touch the human soul and unveil the unconscious psyche" (*Once Upon,* 2).

2. See Sandra M. Gilbert and Susan Gubar, *The Madwoman in the Attic: The Woman Writer and the Nineteenth-Century Imagination* (New Haven: Yale University Press, 1979); Sandra Gilbert, "Life's Empty Pack: Notes Towards a Literary Daughteronomy," *Critical Inquiry* 11, no. 3 (1985), 355–84; Jack Zipes, *Fairy Tales and the Art of Subversion: The Classical Genre for Children and the Process of Civilization* (New York: Methuen, 1983); Ruth B. Bottigheimer, "Silenced Women in the Grimms' Tales: The 'Fit' Between Fairy Tales and Society in Their Historical Context" in her *Fairy Tales and Society,* 115–32, hereafter cited in the text; and her subsequent book, *Grimms' Bad Girls and Bold Boys: The Moral and Social Vision of the Tales* (New Haven: Yale University Press, 1987).

CHAPTER 3

1. For a discussion of the stylistic transformations of oral stories into written documents, see my article "In Defense of the

Grimms: The Aesthetics of Style in Oral and Printed Folktale Texts," *Southern Folklore* 48 (1991), 255–74.

2. Linda Dégh, "Grimm's *Household Tales* and Its Place in the Household," *Western Folklore* 38 (1979), 83–103; Maria Tatar, *The Hard Facts of the Grimms' Fairy Tales* (Princeton: Princeton University Press, 1987), hereafter cited in the text; Bottigheimer, *Bad Girls and Bold Boys.*

3. The specific texts and publishing information for these authors are listed under "Recommended Titles."

4. Jonathan Swift, *Gulliver's Travels* (New York: Lancer Books, 1968).

5. Boris Artzybasheff, ed., *Aesop's Fables* (New York: Viking Press, 1933); Jean de la Fontaine, *The Fables of La Fontaine,* trans. Marianne Moore (New York: Viking Press, 1954).

6. Kenneth Grahame, *The Wind in the Willows* (New York: Scribner's, 1983); George Orwell, *Animal Farm* (New York: Harcourt Brace, 1954); Richard Adams, *Watership Down* (New York: Macmillan, 1972).

7. Rudyard Kipling, *Just So Stories for Little Children* (New York: Doubleday, 1902); Thornton W. Burgess, *Mother West Wind "How" Stories* (Boston: Little, Brown, & Co., 1927).

8. *Panchatantra,* trans. Arthur W. Ryder (Chicago: University of Chicago Press, 1925).

9. Somadeva Bhatta, *The Katha savit sagara; or Ocean of the Streams of Story,* trans. C. H. Tawney (Delhi: Munshiran Manoharlal, 1968).

10. *The Arabian Nights' Entertainments, or The Thousand and One Nights,* coll. and ed. Andrew Lang (London: Longman's, Green, 1898).

11. *The Mabinogian,* trans. Geoffrey Gantz (New York: Penguin, 1976).

12. Geoffrey Chaucer, *The Canterbury Tales,* trans. Neville Coghill, 2 vols. (London: Folio Society, 1956–57).

13. Giovanni Boccaccio, *Decameron,* the John Payne translation, revised and annotated by Charles S. Singleton (Berkeley: University of California Press, 1982); Giovanni Francesco

Straparola, *The Facetious Nights (Le piacevoli notti,* also known as *The Pleasureful Nights* or *The Pleasant Nights),* trans. W. G. Waters (London: Society of Bibliophiles, 1898).

14. Charles Perrault, *Contes du Ma Mere L'Oye; Histoires ou Contes du Temps Passe; avec des Moralites,* trans. A. E. Johnson and others in *Complete Fairy Tales* (New York: Dodd, Mead, 1961).

15. Madame Marie Catherine Jumelle de Berneville, comtesse d'Aulnoy, *La Chatte blanche,* adapted by Leonard B. Lubin (Boston: Little, Brown, & Co., 1978); Madame de Beaumont, *Beauty and the Beast,* trans. Diane Goode (Scarsdale, N.Y.: Bradbury Press, 1978).

16. J. K. Musaus, *Volksmärchen der Deutschen* (Leipzig: F. A. Bookhaus, 1868), first published in 1782.

17. See the section "Analyses of the Grimms' Collection" in the "Bibliographic Essay."

18. Edgar Allan Poe, *The Fall of the House of Usher,* ed. Eric W. Carlson (Columbus, Ohio: Merrill, 1971); Poe, *Poems* (Charlottesville: University Press of Virginia, 1965).

19. Herman Melville, *The Confidence Man: His Masquerade* (Indianapolis: Bobbs-Merrill, 1967).

20. Mark Twain, *The Adventures of Huckleberry Finn,* illus. Barry Moser (Berkeley: University of California Press, 1985); *The Adventures of Tom Sawyer* (Berkeley: University of California Press, 1980); *A Connecticut Yankee in King Arthur's Court* (Berkeley: University of California Press, 1979).

21. Jack Zipes, *Spells of Enchantment: The Wondrous Fairy Tales of Western Culture* (New York: Viking, 1992). See also his analysis of the German literary fairy tale in *Breaking the Magic Spell: Radical Theories of Folk and Fairy Tales* (Austin: University of Texas Press, 1979).

CHAPTER 4

1. Thompson cites two important studies of this fairy tale: Antti Aarne, *Der reiche Mann und sein Schwiegersohn,* FF Communications No. 23, 115–94; and Tille, *Zeitschrift des Vereins für Volkskunde* 29 (1920), 22ff. (*Types of the Folktale,* 157).

2. Thompson identifies two major studies of this fairy tale: Erich Rösch, *Der Getreue Johannes*, FF Communications No. 77; and Kaarle Krohn's essay in FF Communication No. 96, 82ff. (*Types of the Folktale*, 184).

CHAPTER 5

1. Contributions to the feminist perspective on fairy tales are reviewed in the section "Sociohistorical and Feminist Approaches" in the "Bibliographic Essay."

2. *The Complete Grimms Fairy Tales*, 404–11; Lucius Apuleius, *The Transformations of Lucius: Otherwise Known as The Golden Ass*, trans. Jack Lindsay (Bloomington: Indiana University Press, 1960). The story of "Cupid and Psyche" is retold in Edith Hamilton, *Mythology* (New York: Mentor, 1957).

3. Steven Swann Jones, "The Innocent Persecuted Heroine Genre: An Analysis of Its Structure and Themes," *Western Folklore* 52 (1993): 13–42.

4. The only previous study cited by Thompson is Waldemar Liungman's *Sveriges Samtliga Folksagor*, 3 vols. (Stockholm, Sweden: Lindfors Bokforlag, 1949–52), 184ff. (*Types of the Folktale*, 191).

5. Available in English in Andrew Lang, *The Blue Fairy Book* (London: Longman's, Green, 1889), which offers a retelling of the version of "Beauty and the Beast" by Madame de Villeneuve; Lang's text is reprinted in *The Riverside Anthology of Children's Literature*, ed. Judith Saltman (Boston: Houghton Mifflin, 1985), 284–92. The tale type has been well studied; there are nearly two dozen citations concerning this tale type in the last five issues of the MLA bibliography (1986–91). Curiously, the other tale types discussed here (AT 461, 516, and 533) appear not to have received much recent critical attention. Of the many studies of "Beauty and the Beast," two recent discussions worth consulting are Betsy Hearne, *Beauty and the Beast: Visions and Revisions of an Old Tale* (Chicago: University of Chicago Press, 1989); and Maria Tatar, *Off with Their Heads: Fairy Tales and the Culture of Childhood* (Princeton: Princeton University Press, 1992), chapter 7, "Beauties and Beasts," 140–62.

6. Peter Christen Asbjörnsen, *Popular Tales from the Norse,* trans. G. W. Dasent (New York: Putnam's, 1908); reprinted in Saltman, ed. *Riverside Anthology,* 381–86.

CHAPTER 6

1. L. Frank Baum, *The Wizard of Oz* (New York: Penguin, Puffin Books, 1982); Dr. Seuss (Theodore Seuss Geisel), *The Cat in the Hat* (New York: Random House, 1957); Maurice Sendak, *Where the Wild Things Are* (New York: Harper and Row, 1963).

2. Carlo Collodi (pseudonym of Carlo Lorenzini), *The Adventures of Pinocchio,* trans. Carol Della Chiesa (New York: Macmillan, 1969).

Bibliographic Essay

There have been many important contributions to the study of fairy tales since the inception of folklore as an academic discipline at the start of the nineteenth century. In this section I will undertake to survey some of the most significant studies that have influenced the way we understand the genre of the fairy tale. These entries will be presented under two main topics areas—the Classification of fairy tales and the interpretation of fairy tales—and then further subdivided as appropriate.

The Classification of Fairy Tales

It is fitting that Jacob and Wilhelm Grimm begin this survey, since their efforts (published between 1812 and 1815) to record ....the archaic German language in the old stories of the folk represented one of the first systematic studies of fairy tales as they circulate in oral tradition. This first edition of their collection is entitled *Kinder- und Hausmärchen: Gesammelt durch die Brüder Grimm* and is available in a 1986 text edited by Heinze Rölleke (Göttingen: Vandenhoek & Ruprecht). It contains 211 texts, many of which are versions of classic fairy tales. Wilhelm subsequently edited this collection extensively, and six additional editions were published over the next 30 years.

The Grimm's collection of fairy tales has served as the impetus for, as well as the source and subject matter of, much fairy tale research (see the subheading of "Analyses of the Grimms' Collection" in the next section on interpretation of fairy tales). Initially, it contributed to the process of classifying fairy tales. Antti Aarne's attempt to classify fairy tales as well as other folktales, entitled *Verzeichnis der Marchentypen* (FF Communications No. 3, Helsinki, 1910) was based on the Grimms' tales and even used the numbers they assigned to the tales as a way of referring to them. Aarne's index bears major responsibility for our initial awareness of both the breadth of this genre as well as the essential characteristics of the tales. In defining popular fairy tale types and describing these tales by their primary action traits, Aarne began the process of identifying the essential elements of fairy tales. In a companion study, *Leitfaden der verfleichenden Marchenforschung* (FF Communications No. 13, Hamina, 1913) he articulated some of the laws of oral transmission governing folktales and fairy tales. He was following the lead of Axel Olrik, who in 1908 had published "The Epic Laws of Folk Narrative" (available in English translation in Alan Dundes, *The Study of Folklore* [Englewood, N.J.: Prentice Hall, 1965], 129–41).

Johannes Bolte and Georg Polívka's five-volume *Anmerkungen zu den Kinder- und Hausmärchen der Brüder Grimm* (Leipzig: Dieterichsche Verlagsbuchhandlung, 1913–32) also used the Grimms' collection as a starting point for cataloging fairy tales. Their study is a massive compilation of all the analogues they could find to the tales in the Grimms' collection, and it amounted to one of the first attempts to document fairy tales as they exist in multiple versions.

In 1928 (FF Communications No. 74, published by the Finnish Academy of Science in Helsinki) and then again in 1961 in *The Types of the Folktale; A Classification and Bibliography* (FF Communications No. 184, Helsinki), Stith Thompson (listing Aarne as first author) translated and enlarged Aarne's initial work, expanding it ultimately to include some 2,000 tale types (that is, he produced a catalog of the plots of various kinds of folktales, such as jokes, romantic tales, animal fables, and fairy tales) and assigned type numbers 300 to 749 to fairy tales, such as "Cinderella" (Aarne-Thompson type 510). This revised 1961 edition is essential to any fairy tale research. It offers synopses of the individual tale types, a bibliography of major studies of each type, as well as a catalog of extant versions available in written form (many from European archives).

Stith Thompson's companion text, *The Folktale* (New York: Holt, Reinhart, and Winston, 1946) is arguably the most important study in English of the fairy tale. While Thompson includes as folktales a wide variety of folk narrative (including some myths, legends, and animal fables and some realistic folktales), nonetheless it offers the most comprehensive survey available of the various fairy tales that make up this genre. It also offers reviews of folktale scholarship and methodology up to its publication date (which are by now mostly of historical interest).

Stith Thompson also compiled the *Motif-Index of Folk-Literature* (Bloomington: Indiana University Press, 1955–58), a six-volume listing of the major motifs that recur in fairy tales and other folk narratives.

THE HISTORIC-GEOGRAPHIC SCHOOL

The Aarne-Thompson type index is indebted to the methods of the historic-geographic school. Walter Anderson's 1923 study, *Kaiser und Abt: Die Geschichte eines Schwanks* (FF Communications No. 42, Helsinki) was one of the first and most complete illustrations of the benefits of this method. Anderson attempted to document all known versions of the tale type known as "The King and the Abbot" (AT 922) and to trace its historical and geographical development. Similarly, his 1951 study, *Ein volkskundliches Experiments* (FF Communications No. 141, Helsinki) also tried to explain the way that fairy tales are disseminated in oral tradition according to the principles of the historic-geographic school.

Kaarle Krohn, in his 1926 study *Die folkloristische Arbeitsmethode*, trans. Roger L. Welsch, *Folklore Methodology* (Austin: University of Texas Press, 1971), provided a thorough articulation of the principles and procedures of the historic-geographic approach. His study explains how, by using this approach, scholars can systematically identify the action traits of fairy tales and other folktales, and then chart the spread of the tales historically and geographically.

The valuable studies of fairy tales employing the historic-geographic method are simply too numerous to mention in this brief bibliographic survey. Many of them, such as Archer Taylor's *The Black Ox* (FF Communications No. 70, Helsinki, 1927), may be found among the more than 250 monographs published by Folklore Fellows Communications (Helsinki: Academia Scientiarum Fennica, available through the Soumalainen Tiedeakatemia bookstore). Another especially useful study, Warren Roberts's *The Tale of the Kind and Unkind Girls*, was published by *Fabula* (as a supplement in 1958 in Berlin by de Gruyter).

Carl von Sydow was a critic of the historic-geographic approach. He felt that fairy tales were disseminated by individual narrators, gifted storytellers (he called them "active bearers of tradition"), who carried their repertoires with them. Thus, the tales did not spread like the ripples of a stone thrown into a pond (a favorite analogy of the historic-geographic school), but rather skipped and jumped around as various narrators moved to different countries. He also argued that tales frequently manifested themselves as *oikotypes*, that is, regionally localized and specialized versions of traditional tale types. He suggested, therefore, that placing versions in their appropriate ethnic community is crucial. His theories are presented in *Selected Papers on Folklore*, ed. Laurits Bodker (Copenhagen: Rosenkilde and Bagger, 1948).

Despite von Sydow's criticisms, the concept of the tale type has flourished, and various scholars have compiled indexes of individual types as well as of various genres or geographical samples of these types. Two important such surveys include Ernest Böklen's *Sneewittchenstudien*, Mythologische Bibliothek, vols. 3 and 7 (Leipzig: J. C. Hinrichs, 1910, 1915) and Anna Brigitta Rooth's *The Cinderella Cycle* (Lund: Gleerup, 1951). The former surveys nearly 100 versions of "Snow White," while the latter summarizes many hundreds of versions of "Cinderella."

May Augusta Klipple's 1938 study, *African Folk Tales with Foreign Analogues* (Bloomington: Indiana University Press), employs the classification system proposed by Aarne and helps to define the traditional European fairy tales identified by Aarne by showing how they were carried to Africa and then told and retold by European immigrants and missionaries. She also identifies some indigenous African tales that resemble European tales closely enough to raise questions about which continent those tales may have originated in.

Another compendium of fairy tales of value to folklorists is Katherine Briggs's two-volume *A Dictionary of British Folk-Tales in the English Language* (Bloomington: Indiana University Press, 1970–71), which presents many summaries of popular tale types circulating in the British Isles.

Terrence L. Hansen employed the Aarne and Thompson index of folktales in *The Types of the Folktale in Cuba, Puerto-Rico, Dominican Republic and Spanish South America* (Berkeley and Los Angeles: University of California Folklore Studies, no. 8, 1957). And Ernest W. Baughman also used the Aarne and Thompson classficatory scheme in *Type and Motif-Index of the Folktales of England and North America* (Bloomington: Indiana University Folklore Series, no. 20, 1966). There are many other such indexes of folktales from various parts of the world that can be used to identify fairy tales circulating in those regions.

Daniel J. Crowley's 1966 study *I Could Talk Old-Story Good: Creativity in Bahamian Folklore* (Folklore Studies 17, Berkeley: University of California Press) also works from Aarne's classification, but he offers a different perspective on the multiplicity of fairy tales circulating in oral tradition. In Crowley's view, the fundamental building blocks of fairy tales are not the types, which he finds frequently altered, but rather the motifs that are recombined in oral tradition in many different plots.

In contrast, D. L. Ashliman finds the Aarne and Thompson concept of the tale type useful and has compiled *A Guide to Folktales in the English Language* (Westport: Greenwood Press, 1987), which catalogs the appearance of the traditional Aarne-Thompson tale types in major folktale collections available in English. Another useful catalog of fairy tale sources is Mary Huse Eastman's *Index to Fairy Tales, Myths, and Legends,* published by Faxon initially in 1926, with supplements in 1937 and 1952. In 1973 and 1979, Norma Olin Ireland provided updated supplements for 1949–72 and 1973–77.

THE STRUCTURAL APPROACH

Vladimir Propp in his 1928 study, *Morfologija skazki* (Leningrad, trans. as *Morphology of the Folktale* [Austin: University of Texas Press, 1968]), is credited with first bringing the methods of structural analysis to the classification of fairy tales. He suggests that the functions of the tales' dramatis personae can be reduced to their fundamental essence, and thus a basic pattern of action can be deduced. He concludes that one basic plot outline characterizes all fairy tales. His title and thesis attempt to indicate his discovery of the essential morphology (shape or form) of the wonder or fairy tale.

Actually, Propp was preceded by and presumably indebted to Alexandr Isaakovich Nikiforov, who was part of a common research group with Propp and who published in 1927, a year before Propp's study, "On the Morphological Study of Folklore." Part of the reason for Nikiforov's neglect is that he did not go on to publish a book on the subject of structural folktale classification, and his Russian article was not translated into English until 1973 (by Heda Jason in *Linguistica Biblica*, vols. 27–28: 25–35). His insights about how fairy tales are structured not only predate Propp's but are more sophisticated and better. Unlike Propp's Procrustean reduction of all fairy tales to a single plot paradigm, Nikiforov more logically identifies a number of basic tale outlines: a male fairy-tale pattern, a gender-neutral pattern, and a female fairy-tale pattern that has two predominant schemes, tales about winning a groom and tales about an unjustly persecuted maiden or woman.

Heda Jason has advocated the structural analysis of fairy tales, not only in her translating of Nikiforov's important article, but also in articles such as "The Russian Criticism of the 'Finnish school' in Folktale Scholarship," *Norveg,* vol. 14 (1970): 287–94, and "Structural Analysis and the Concept of the 'Tale-Type,'" *ARV*, vol. 28 (1972): 36–54. In addition, she coedited with Dmitri M. Segal an important collection of essays, *Patterns in Oral Literature* (Paris/The Hague: Mouton, 1977).

Alan Dundes followed Propp in his criticism of the classificatory method underlying the historic-geographic school, in particular challenging its identification of motifs as essential elements of tale types. This principle is employed in Aarne and Thompson's index of folktales and results in the description of tale types by concrete elements that might not be in a given selected version. In his 1962 study, "From Etic to Emic Units in the Structural Study of Folktales" (*Journal of American Folklore,* vol. 75: 95–105) as well as in his 1964 publication of his dissertation, *The Morphology of North American Indian Folktales* (FF

Communications No. 195, Helsinki), Dundes suggests that a better system of classification would be one based on fundamental generic structures of various kinds of folktales. While he follows Propp's theory in this regard, he does not support Propp's conclusions concerning the morphological structure of the fairy tale as a genre. Dundes suggests instead some other generic patterns for folktales, such as interdiction followed by violation of the interdiction, or identification of a lack of some sort followed by the acquisition of whatever is lacking. While these patterns seem to characterize some American Indian folktales, they have not as yet been used to help us to define traditional European fairy tales.

My own 1983 essay, "The Structure of *Snow White*" (*Fabula*, vol. 24: 56–71), attempted to combine the historic-geographic focus on individual tale types with the structural method of identifying essential, generalized actions characterizing specific tale types. I identify nine basic "episodes" (origin, jealousy, expulsion, adoption, renewed jealousy, death, exhibition, resuscitation, and resolution) that appear to underlie the fundamental plot of "Snow White" and conclude that the concept of the tale type is valid and can be best defined by the structural analysis of the component episodes. I offered a similar analysis entitled "Structural and Thematic Applications of the Comparative Method: A Case Study of 'The Kind and Unkind Girls'" in the *Journal of Folklore Research*, vol. 23 (1986): 148–61.

Interpretation

The interpretation of fairy tales has been a lively and controversial practice for many centuries. Initially, the fascination with where these stories came from resulted not just in attempts to establish their origins and paths of dissemination, but also in the creation of elaborate theories to explain their often bizarre and apparently nonsensical imagery. For example, some scholars proposed the theory that fairy tales were the cultural debris of earlier, more sophisticated, and culturally advanced societies that were remembered but little understood by the folk that used them. Such a hypothesis is argued by Albert Wesselski in his 1931 study *Versuch einer Theorie des Märchens* (Prager Deutsche

Studien 45; Reichenberg: Kraus). And Wilhelm Grimm, in his introductions to various editions of the Grimms' collection, voices this outlook to some extent. Related to this theory was the notion that the tales were all the product of a common Indo-European culture, both in language and in significance. Stith Thompson summarizes these early approaches nicely: "1) the circle of those tales which show close resemblances is coterminous with the Indo-European language family and these tales are doubtless inheritances from a common Indo-European antiquity; 2) the tales are broken down myths and are to be understood only by a proper interpretation of the myths from which they came. These pronouncements give expression to what is generally known as 1) the Indo-European theory, 2) the broken-down myth theory" (370).

Related to both of these theories was another that more specifically suggested that the subject of the original Indo-European myths which eventually deteriorated into fairy tales was nature and, in particular, the solar cycle. These scholars were called solar mythologists, and they linked the fairy tales to primitive rituals celebrating the return of the sun each morning and every spring. These theories have by now become so out-of-date that full citation of the various scholars who proposed them is unnecessary. If one were interested, Thompson offers a thorough overview of them in part 4 of *The Folktale*, and Richard Dorson provides a historical review of their contributions in "The Eclipse of Solar Mythology," in Thomas A. Sebeok, "Myth: A Symposium" (*Journal of American Folklore*, vol. 68 [1968]: 379–495) as well as in *The British Folklorists* (Chicago: University of Chicago Press, 1968).

THE ANTHROPOLOGICAL APPROACH

As the prehistoric nature of many of these tales became established, and thus precluded definitive conclusions about the creation of fairy tales, the critical focus of scholars changed from the origin of the stories to their function. Anthropology scholars such as Andrew Lang analyzed how these stories and other folk narratives functioned in contemporary oral tradition. Lang's views are found in *Custom and Myth* (New York: Harper Bros., 1885) and in various reviews and introductions, such as the one he wrote for Marian R. Cox's *Cinderella: Three Hundred and Forty-Five Variants of Cinderella, Catskin, and Cap o' Rushes* (London: Publications of the Folklore Society, no. 26, 1890). Lang worked from E. B. Tylor's *Primitive Culture*, 2 vols. (London: John Murray, 1871), which was one of the first attempts to record scientifically the way primitive culture used its traditions, including literature.

Others who shared this anthropological approach included Sir James G. Frazer, *The Golden Bough* (London: Macmillan, 1907–15), Arnold van Gennep, *The Rites of Passage* (Chicago: University of Chicago Press, 1960), and Bronislaw Malinowski, *Myth in Primitive Psychology* (New York: W. W. Norton and Co., 1926) and *Magic, Science, and Religion, and Other Essays* (Boston: Beacon Press, 1948).

The analysis of fairy tales in the context of anthropological assessment of their host culture led to studies such as Alfred Winterstein's 1928 article, "Die Pubertätsriten der Mädchen und ihre Spuren im Märchen," *Imago*, vol. 14: 199–274, one of the first essays to point out the connection between fairy tales and social rituals. Further research into the ritual basis of fairy tales has been spurred by Victor Turner's work *The Ritual Process: Structure and Anti-Structure* (Ithaca, N.Y.: Correll University Press, 1977).

PSYCHOLOGICAL INTERPRETATION

A third major approach to the interpretation of fairy tales (after the "broken-down myth" theory and contemporaneous with the anthropological school) is the psychological approach. Sigmund Freud, initially in *Interpretation of Dreams* (originally published in German in 1900, translated by James Strachey, New York: Avon Books, 1965) as well as throughout his later studies, such as *The Occurrence in Dreams of Material from Fairy Tales* (London: Hogarth Press, 1913) and his coauthored study with D. E. Oppenheim, "Dreams in Folklore," in the *Standard Edition of the Complete Psychological Works of Sigmund Freud,* trans. James Strachey, ed. Anna Freud et al. (London: Hogarth, 1959), vol. 12, 177–211, suggested that the much of the imagery and content of fairy tales was drawn directly from the dreams and unconscious minds of audiences. Freud's analysis of the tale of Oedipus (which is actually a legend in that Oedipus is a king of Thebes and the story ends unhappily) connected that story to the child's rivalry with the parent of the same sex and the child's emotional obsession with the parent of the opposite sex. Numerous scholars have applied this idea to various fairy tales, for example, A. S. Macquisten and R. W. Pickford in "Psychological Aspects of the Fantasy of Snow White and the Seven Dwarfs," *Psychoanalytic Review,* vol. 29 (1942): 233–252. This journal, as well as other journals in psychology, have published many such analyses of fairy tales from depth-psychological perspectives. Alexander Grinstein's *Index of Psychoanalytic Writings* (New York: International Universities Press, 1956–75) is a useful bibliographic tool to help track down these studies.

An early proponent of the psychological approach to folktale interpretation (as well as ritual and other forms of folklore) was Ernest Jones. His *Essays in Applied Psychoanalysis* (London: Hogarth, 1951) provides many illuminating psychological insights into folk narratives. Similarly, in *The Gates of the Dream* (New York: International Universities Press, 1952) as well as in various essays, such as "Fairy Tale and Dream" in *The Psychoanalytic Study of the Child,* vol. 8, ed. Ruth S. Eissler et al. (New York: International Universities Press, 1953), 394–403, and "Dame Holle: Dream and Folktale" in *Explorations in Psychoanalysis,* ed. Robert Lindner (New York: Julian Press, 1953), 84–94, Géza Róheim points out the connection between fairy tales and dream psychology.

One of the most popular applications of the psychological approach to fairy tales was Erich Fromm's *The Forgotten Language: An Introduction to the Understanding of Dreams, Fairy Tales and Myths* (New York: Rinehart, 1951). His approach to the baffling language of fairy tales suggests it harkens back to pre-conscious memories and primal experiences. Julius Heuscher, in *A Psychiatric Study of Myths and Fairy Tales* (Springfield: Charles C Thomas, 1974), also offers a psychoanalytic reading of various fairy tales. He sees them as offering a primer of child psychology and as assisting the child in the process of self-actualization.

Bruno Bettelheim's *The Uses of Enchantment* (New York: Random House, Vintage Books, 1976) also focuses on the psychological significance of fairy tales for children. He works from many of Freud's concepts (such as the oedipal complex) and analyzes how the Grimms' versions of many popular fairy tales might symbolically depict emotional anxieties experienced by children. In particular, he discusses the depiction of oedipal and existential anxieties in the tales.

Alan Dundes has also applied the psychological approach to the study of fairy tales. In his 1975 collection, *Analytic Essays in Folklore* (The Hague: Mouton), he offers readings of various tales to show how they illustrate unconscious concerns. A subsequent essay, "'To love my father all': A Psychoanalytic Study of the Folktale Source of *King Lear*," *Southern Folklore Quarterly*, vol. 40 (1976): 353–66, discusses the oedipal theme in "The Maiden Without Hands" (AT 706) and "Love Like Salt" (AT 923) and their connection to Shakespeare's play.

Another seminal figure in the psychological analysis of fairy tales was Carl Jung. In his collected works, especially in *Symbols of Transformation* and *The Archetypes and the Collective Unconscious*, vol. 5 and vol. 9, respectively, of *The Collected Works of C. G. Jung*, ed. by William McGuire (Princeton: Princeton University Press, 1970), Jung suggests that the symbolic imagery of fairy tales may be viewed as depicting the exploration of the unconscious mind. In journeying into a fantastic realm, the protagonist, according to Jung, is journeying into his or her own unconscious to confront the psychological conflicts festering there. Jung also identified various traditional characters of fairy tales as corresponding to basic types of people audiences are familiar with, such as a mother archetype, a child archetype, or a trickster archetype. He coauthored with Karl Kerenyi *Essays on a Science of Mythology: The Myths of the Divine Child and the Divine Maiden* (New York: Harper & Row, 1949), which offers an analysis of two such types. Jung felt that these types and other fundamental components of fairy tales were part of the "collective unconscious," that is, part of a racial memory passed down genetically from previous generations.

Marie-Louise von Franz offers a psychological analysis with a Jungian emphasis in *Interpretation of Fairy Tales: An Introduction to the Psychology of Fairy Tales* (Zurich: Spring Publications, 1970) as well as in *Problems of the Feminine in Fairy Tales* (New York: Spring Publications, 1972) and *Shadow and Evil in Fairy Tales* (Zurich: Spring Publications, 1974).

Joseph Campbell in *The Hero with a Thousand Faces* (Princeton: Princeton University Press, 1970) adopts Jung's concept of the

exploration of the unconscious by fairy tale protagonists. He analyzes how various fairy tales, among other narratives, illustrate
the confrontation of basic fears and anxieties (about parent figures, approaching sexual maturation and responsibilities, death)
through their symbolic imagery. He emphasizes how the plots of
most fairy tales may be seen as depicting a psychological process
(which Jung identified and labeled integration or individuation),
which involves the reconciliation of the conscious and unconscious minds by means of a direct exploration by the protagonist
of the hidden contents of the unconscious mind. According to
this theory, by symbolically facing the exaggerated fears of the
unconscious, the fairy tale protagonist learns to accept and overcome them.

Another scholar who recognizes the essentially symbolic
nature of fairy tales is Max Lüthi. He has been one of the most
prolific, as well as illuminating, critics of the fairy tale. In his early
study *The European Folktale: Form and Nature,* trans. John D. Niles
(Bloomington: Indiana University Press, 1982), as well as in *Once
Upon a Time: On the Nature of Fairy Tales,* trans. Lee Chadeayne
and Paul Gottwald (Bloomington: Indiana University Press,
1970) and *The Fairy Tale as Art Form and Portrait of Man,* trans. Jon
Erickson (Bloomington: Indiana University Press, 1984), Lüthi
argues that the abstract style of the fairy tale is its most essential
characteristic. For Lüthi, this abstract style is a reflection of the
fairy tale's symbolic nature: "Unconsciously, or semiconsciously,
[listeners] do not regard the images that fill their mind's eye to be
merely pictures, but always metaphors as well. In is only when
the image is consciously interpreted that its poetic effect is
destroyed. . . . [These images] are representatives of the visible
world of the cosmos and of human affairs. But they may also signify facets of the unconscious inner world of human beings.
What is unconscious and ineffable finds visible expression in
them. In this sense, they are not symbols that conceal, but symbols that reveal" (*The European Folktale,* 94–95). Lüthi thus echoes
not only the psychological perspective of many other fairy tale
scholars, he also is one of the first to articulate the epistemological basis of the exotic symbolism of fairy tales. The abstract style
he documents so fully is the product of the symbolic or analogical perspective of the human mind, reflecting its ability to see the
world from a poetic point of view.

A particularly popular study is Clarissa Pinkola Estes's *Women Who Run with the Wolves: Myths and Stories of the Wild Woman Archetype* (New York: Ballantine Books, 1992). A Jungian disciple, Estes offers extensive discussions of "Bluebeard," "Vasilisa," "Manawee," "The Ugly Duckling," "The Red Shoes," "Sealskin, Soulskin," "La Llorona," "The Little Match Girl," "The Three Golden Hairs," "The Woman with Hair of Gold," and "The Handless Maiden" as illustrations of the archetype of the wild woman and the ordeals that women endure. Her book is praise-worthy on two counts—she is a wonderful storyteller, providing splendid versions of some classic fairy tales, and she offers read-ers an emotionally uplifting psychological outlook. She finds fairy tales dramatizing the condition and travails of women and offering them encouragement and support. On the other hand, the book seems blithely unaware of the critiques of fairy tales articulated by feminists such as Sandra Gilbert, who do not regard the linking of women in fairy tales with instinctive and supernatural powers in an entirely positive light (see the discus-sion of studies by Sandra Gilbert and Cristina Bacchilega under the subsequent section on sociohistorical and feminist approach-es). In comparison to Gilbert's analysis of "Allerleirauh," Estes's discussion of "The Handless Maiden" seems rather superficial and unconvincing.

Following Freud's and especially Jung's seminal psychological theories, numerous studies have used fairy tales to illustrate their psychological analyses. Not only do fairy tales seem ripe material for psychological exegesis, they have become a common point of reference for these discussions. Limitations of space, however, prevent me from reviewing all of these psychological studies that use fairy tales incidentally to illustrate their theories. Recent studies by three scholars do deserve mention, though. Allan B. Chinen has contributed *In the Ever After: Fairy Tales and the Second Half of Life* (Wilmette, Ill.: Chiron Publications, 1989) and *Once Upon a Midlife: Classical Stories and Mythic Tales to Illuminate the Middle Years* (Los Angeles: Jeremy P. Tarcher, 1992). As I indicate in the body of my study, Chinen's work is valuable not only for its application of psychological theory to fairy tales, but also because it identifies two subgenres of fairy tales, those for elders and those for middle-aged adults. He sees certain specific fairy tales functioning to assist individuals in coping with unconscious anxieties related to middle and old age. Another influential study is Robert Bly's *Iron John: A Book About Men* (New York: Vintage, 1992). He sees fairy tales as offering men help in their struggles to understand themselves.

THE STRUCTURAL APPROACH

Another method for interpreting fairy tales (as opposed to seeing certain psychological ideas or themes as prevalent in the stories) is to see what patterns or structures, what social or epistemological paradigms they convey. The essence of this approach is to look for abstract or generalized patterns in various stories and then to interpret them in order to reveal what the shared focus of that pattern may be.

For example, Campbell's work may also be seen as following a structural approach, in addition to his psychological orientation. *The Hero with a Thousand Faces* suggests that a wide variety of fairy tales, myths, and religious narratives all share what he calls the "monomyth," a single plot outline that includes a call to adventure, a threshold crossing (into another realm that represents the unconscious as well as the supernatural dimension), various tests and helpers, a climactic confrontation, a boon, a return crossing, and a reincorporation of the protagonist back into society. Campbell shows how this pattern recurs in many different narratives, especially fairy tales, and then goes on to suggest that the pattern is representative not only of the inward journey of the exploration of the unconscious mind, but also of the outward journey of the exploration of the mystery of the universe, its supernatural realm. He also links this pattern to Arnold van Gennep's theory of the pattern of separation, initiation, and return, as presented in *The Rites of Passage* (Chicago: University of Chicago Press, 1960), which van Gennep says characterizes many rituals. The purpose of this pattern in these rituals is to facilitate transition between various social roles, which could also be part of its function in the fairy tales. The structural approach looks for patterns first, and then draws connections to the social issues and personal concerns that might link these tales to their audiences (rather than assuming that the tales are intrinsically about certain psychological or social or spiritual themes at the outset).

Claude Lévi-Strauss argues for a structural approach to the interpretation of folk narrative, particularly in his 1955 essay "The Structural Study of Myth" (*Journal of American Folklore*, vol. 68: 428–45). There he suggests that thematic meanings could be derived from the bundles of alternative motifs employed in different versions of the Oedipus legend.

Alan Dundes also argues for a structural approach to folktale interpretation. In "The Symbolic Equivalence of Allomotifs in the Rabbit Herd (AT 570)" (*ARV*, vol. 36 [1980]: 91–98), as well as in "The Symbolic Equivalence of Allomotifs: Towards a Method of Analyzing Folktales" in Genevieve Calame-Griaule et. al., *Le Conte, pourqui? comment? / Folktales, Why and How?* (Paris: Mouton, 1984), 187–99, Dundes proposes the idea of analyzing the "allomotifs" (the range of alternately used motifs in a given folktale) of a tale type to reveal thematic and symbolic continuities.

My own study, *The New Comparative Method: Structural and Symbolic Analysis of the Allomotifs of "Snow White"* (FF Communications No. 247; Helsinki: Academia Scientiarum Fennica, 1990) applies this methodology to an interpretation of that fairy tale. The variation in motifs introduced by storytellers (such as having Snow White be killed by a poisoned corset, stay-lace, comb, broach, dress, ring, slippers, grape, raisin, magic dehydrating seed, or apple) can help us to understand the underlying symbolic significance of her death. The items all have to do with her beautification as a woman or with her ingestion of a seed or fruit, revealing a focus on the heroine's physical and sexual maturation, inasmuch as the beautification signals her readiness for a mate, and the ingestion of some sort of seed is metaphoric of her acknowledging the idea and principle of reproduction.

SOCIOHISTORICAL AND FEMINIST APPROACHES

These two approaches are linked in that they attempt to connect fairy tales to the value systems and cultural proclivities of the communities in which the tales circulate. From this perspective, the tales are seen as reflections of (as well as promulgators of) cultural norms. These approaches may be regarded as offshoots of the anthropological school, inasmuch as the cultural context of the tales assumes primacy in attempting to derive interpretations of their meaning (as opposed to psychological themes or philosophical paradigms). Placing a tale in its proper cultural context and knowing intimately the nuances of that culture's beliefs, values, social roles, and norms is crucial from the point of view of these scholars. They differ from the anthropological approach in that the focus is not exclusively on how these tales operate in a primitive society. The anthropological approach tends to regard these tales as existing authentically only in nonliterate societies, whereas the sociohistorical approach analyzes the tales as they exist in any society. For a bibliographic overview of both the social and psychological perspectives on fairy tale analysis, one might consult J. L. Fischer's 1963 essay "The Socio-psychological Analysis of Folktales" (*Current Anthropology,* vol. 4: 235–95).

One problem of the sociohistorical approach for fairy tales is that the tale types as a phenomenon generally cross cultural boundaries quite readily and extensively, so determining the appropriate cultural context for a tale found in China, India, and various Mediterranean as well as Eastern and Western European countries is nearly impossible. As a result, this approach tends to focus on individual versions specific to a particular community or storyteller, and glosses over the larger phenomenon of the tale type that circulates among different cultures.

Ironically, perhaps one of the best proponents of the sociohistorical approach is Vladimir Propp. He is better known for having popularized the structural analysis of fairy tales, but his later work is devoted more to placing these tales in a social and historical context, evaluating their inculcation of cultural belief systems. For example, in *Theory and History of Folklore* (Minneapolis: University of Minnesota Press, 1984), which includes a translation of selections from *Historical Roots of the Wondertale* and as well as other works, he argues that the fairy tale research has two parts: generic analysis based on scientific description of the phenomena and historical analysis that connects the phenomena to its ethnographic context. He regards his *Morphology of the Folktale* as having been mistranslated (it should have been *Morphology of the Wondertale*) and misunderstood: it was only the first step to a thorough methodology that moves from synchronic, stylistic, and descriptive analysis to diachronic and ethnographic analysis. He argues ultimately that the plot and composition of the wondertale (fairy tale) are conditioned by a kinship system at the stage of development represented by the American Indian tribes. He also offers a brilliant reading of "The Princess Who Would Not Laugh," connecting it to the function of laughter in procreative and fertility rituals and to the myth of Demeter.

Perhaps the leading exponent of the sociohistorical approach to fairy tale interpretation is Lutz Röhrich. His 1956 study, *Märchen und Wirklichkeit: Eine volkskundliche Untersuchung* (Weisbaden: Steiner), is available in English, translated by Peter Tokofsky as *Folktales and Reality* (Bloomington: Indiana University Press, 1991). It offers a thorough analysis of the rituals and beliefs underlying fairy tales in order to show the tales' connection to the ethnic, social, and historical background of their audiences. As his title indicates, Röhrich is concerned with connecting the magical and fantastic images of fairy tales to literal and historical reality, in particular to the belief systems of the specific audiences.

Another seminal study of fairy tales from a sociohistorical perspective is Linda Dégh's *Folktales and Society: Storytelling in a Hungarian Peasant Community* (Bloomington: Indiana University Press, 1969). She analyzes in detail the narratives told in a particular community to show their relationship to the concerns of that community.

Jack Zipes also argues for a sociohistorical perspective, although his view is considerably broader than Dégh's. He does not look at a specific ethnic community, but rather analyzes the tales in the context of national and cultural preoccupations. For example, in *Fairy Tales and the Art of Subversion: The Classical Genre for Children and the Process of Civilization* (New York: Methuen, 1983), he finds fairy tales perpetuating an elitist, bourgeois, and sexist ideology.

Jack Zipes also has edited a collection of essays entitled *Don't Bet on the Prince: Contemporary Feminist Fairy Tales in North America and England* (New York: Methuen, 1986), in which he not only points out the prevailing sexist orientation of many fairy tales, but also attempts to redress that imbalance by offering some tales that offer alternative models of gendered behavior. This collection includes an essay by Karen Rowe, "Feminism and Fairy Tales" (209–26; reprinted from *Women's Studies*, vol. 6 [1979]: 237–57), that points out how traditional fairy tales perpetuate cultural norms through their depiction of marriage.

Another important collection of studies on fairy tales is Ruth B. Bottigheimer's *Fairy Tales and Society: Illusion, Allusion, and Paradigm* (Philadelphia: University of Pennsylvania Press, 1986). It includes feminist essays by Karen Rowe, "To Spin a Yarn: The Female Voice in Folklore and Fairy Tale," 53–74, and Kay Stone, "Feminist Approaches to the Interpretation of Fairy Tales," 229–34. It includes as well an essay by Jack Zipes, "Marxists and the Illumination of Folk and Fairy Tales," 237–45.

Perhaps the most important articulation of the feminist perspective on fairy tales and literature is Sandra M. Gilbert and Susan Gubar's 1979 study, *The Madwoman in the Attic: The Woman Writer and the Nineteenth-Century Imagination* (New Haven: Yale University Press, 1979). Through their analysis of the representative fairy tale of "Snow White," they argue that the struggle between the queen and Snow White is a battle between the assertive and passive inclinations in all Western women. Snow White's exhibition in the glass coffin represents the victory of her passivity; she has become a beautiful object, to be displayed and desired.

Sandra Gilbert offers another ground-breaking and illuminating analysis in "Life's Empty Pack: Notes Towards a Literary Daughteronomy," *Critical Inquiry,* vol. 11, no. 3 (1985): 355–84. She suggests there that Western women are encouraged in fairy tales and literature to "bury their mothers and marry their fathers," that is, reject their mothers who have been simplistically equated in fairy tales and literature with nature and emotionalism, and identify with the father, who is associated with society, morality, and the patriarchal structure. She analyzes "Allerleirauh" (which is the Grimm's version of AT 510B, "Cap o' Rushes") to show how the heroine, after rejecting marriage with her own father (literal incest), marries instead someone who is just like her father, thereby perpetuating the patriarchal social structure.

Another very interesting and parallel assessment of fairy tales from a feminist perspective is Cristina Bacchilega's "The Fruit of the Womb: Creative Uses of a Naturalizing Tradition in Folktales," in *Creativity and Tradition in Folklore,* ed. Simon Bronner (Logan: Utah State University Press, 1992), 153–66. She points out how women in fairy tales are inevitably linked to and described by natural metaphors, thereby affirming their function as bearers of life but also differentiating them from the men, who are associated with civilization and patriarchal society. Thus, from this view, the fairy tales prescribe and delimit the roles that women may assume.

In addition to those surveyed above, there have been numerous contributions to the feminist analysis of fairy tales that deserve our attention, although limitations of space prevent comment on each one. Some of these include: Madonna Kolbenschlag, *Kiss Sleeping Beauty Good-bye: Breaking the Spell of Feminine Myths and Models* (New York: Doubleday, 1979); Marcia Lieberman, "Some Day My Prince Will Come: Female Acculturation through the Fairy Tale," *College English,* vol. 34 (1972): 383–95; and Kay F. Stone, "The Misuses of Enchantment: Controversies on the Singnificance of Fairy Tales," in *Women's Folklore, Women's Culture,* ed. Rosan A. Jordan and Susan J. Kalcik (Philadephia: University of Pennsylvania Press, 1985), 125–45. These studies show how fairy tales contribute to negative cultural stereotypes for young women.

Not all contemporary sociohistorical studies are feminist. Bengt Holbek offers a thorough review of fairy tale scholarship and methodological options in *Interpretation of Fairy Tales: Danish Folklore in a European Perspective* (FF Communications No. 239, Helsinki, 1987). As his subtitle suggests, he favors an ethnographic approach that analyzes fairy tales in the context of the repertoire of individual narrators and in relation to the community in which those narrators live. Accordingly, he presents an assessment of the tale corpora of five narrators.

Perhaps the greatest attention generated recently for the sociohistorical method has resulted from Robert Darnton's *The Great Cat Massacre and Other Episodes in French Cultural History* (New York: Basic Books, 1984). He argues against the psychological interpretations of fairy tales and contends that "folk tales are historical documents" which require a critical method that looks "for the way a raconteur adapts an inherited theme to his audience, so that the specificity of time and place shows through the universality of the topos" (42). Darnton analyzes a selection of French fairy tales, including "Little Red Riding Hood" ("The Glutton," AT 333), and suggests they communicate a particularly eighteenth-century French ethos and worldview. For a critique of Darnton's ethnocentric preoccupation, see S. Jones, "On

Analyzing Fairy Tales: 'Little Red Riding Hood' Revisited,"
Western Folklore, vol. 46 (1987): 97–106, and Alan Dundes, *Little
Red Riding Hood: A Casebook* (Madison: University of Wisconsin
Press, 1989). See also Jack Zipes's collection of studies and ver-
sions, *The Trials and Tribulations of Little Red Riding Hood: Versions
of the Tale in Sociocultural Context* (South Hadley, Mass.: Bergin &
Garvey, 1983).

A recent contribution to the sociohistorical perspective on
fairy tales is Maria Tatar's *Off with Their Heads: Fairy Tales and the
Culture of Childhood* (Princeton: Princeton University Press, 1992).
Tatar's focus is on how "the fairy tale's surface events often work
in tandem with latent undercurrents to generate the productive
ambiguities that engage our attention as listeners and readers"
(126). The tale's manifest content for Tatar concerns the culturally inscribed notions of what it is to be a child. She contrasts the
didactic attempt by parents and scholars to impose adult lessons
and values on children with the depiction in the tales of what
she considers the children's own desires and concerns.

ANALYSES OF THE GRIMMS' COLLECTION

The Grimms' collection of fairy tales has itself been the subject of
a great deal of scholarship, particularly in German. For example,
many of the essays in the previously cited collection edited by
Ruth B. Bottigheimer, *Fairy Tales and Society*, focus on the
Grimms' tales, including four essays that Bottigheimer translated
from German herself. One of these German essays is by
Germany's leading authority on the Grimms, Heinz Rölleke,
who offers a definitive reassessment of one of the Grimms' storytellers in "The 'Utterly Hessian' Fairy Tales by 'Old Marie': The
End of a Myth" (287–300). He points out that since the informant
known as Marie was actually Marie Hassenpflug, who was a
daughter of a Huguenot family, her versions of the fairy tales
were not especially German.

Bottigheimer herself offers an essay on "Silenced Women in
the Grimms' Tales: The 'Fit' Between Fairy Tales and Society in
Their Historical Context" (115–32), which is drawn from her book
*Grimms' Bad Girls and Bold Boys: The Moral and Social Vision of the
Tales* (New Haven: Yale University Press, 1987). She points out
how much Wilhelm Grimm stylistically altered the texts they collected, deleting dialogue from good female characters and giving

it instead to male characters, evil female characters, or the narrator, thus reinforcing a cultural belief in the value of silent women. In this essay and her book on the Grimms, she advances a sociohistorical and feminist perspective on fairy tales.

Similarly, Linda Dégh's 1979 essay "Grimm's *Household Tales* and Its Place in the Household" (*Western Folklore,* vol. 38: 83–103) argues that the way to understand the Grimms' tales is to examine them in the context of the household storytelling situations in which they functioned.

John M. Ellis offers a somewhat more controversial point of view in his 1983 study, *One Fairy Story Too Many: The Brothers Grimm and Their Tales* (Chicago: University of Chicago Press). He suggests that the Grimms engaged in an Ossian-like deception, passing off literary tales as if they possessed an authentic folkloric heritage. Most scholars of the Grimms (such as Heinz Rölleke) regard this as a somewhat exaggerated claim, since the evidence indicates that the Grimms took considerable pains to collect multiple versions of tales from various oral informants. The Grimm brothers apparently felt that these versions were part of an ongoing oral tradition, even if subsequent scholars such as Ellis and Dégh argue that some of these narratives were actually learned by the informants from books.

Maria Tatar also offers a literary history of the Grimms' collection in her 1987 study *The Hard Facts of the Grimms' Fairy Tales* (Princeton: Princeton University Press). But she comes to different conclusions than Ellis's and advances a different methodology than Bottigheimer's. She details the publishing history of the collection, showing how and why Wilhelm transformed a group of "bawdy tales, hardly acceptable for children" into a sanitized classic of children's literature. She offers an analysis of the editorial changes that Wilhelm introduced over the seven editions of the Grimms' collection, such as adding Christian allusions and deleting scatological references. Her findings are not new, but they do document more fully the extent of the changes incorporated by Wilhelm, changes that are fairly typical of nineteenth-century editorial practices. She recognizes that the Grimms' collection is inherently a product of folk tradition, which includes multiple versions, tale types, and an essentially symbolic language; she questions "who would be so literal minded as to try to explain 'Hansel and Gretel' . . . on realistic terms" (51).

Finally, another valuable collection of fairy tale studies devoted to the Grimms' collection is James M. McGlathery's *The Brothers Grimm and Folktale* (Champaign: University of Illinois Press, 1988). It includes essays on the Grimms' fairy tales such as Linda Dégh's "What Did the Grimm Brothers Give to and Take from the Folk" (66–90) and Heinz Rölleke's "New Results of Research on *Grimms' Fairy Tales*" (101–11).

CONCLUSION

As this survey of fairy tale scholarship indicates, there are many valuable perspectives that one can and should take in studying this genre. As Propp suggests, we must begin with a systematic and logical identification of the phenomenon, and the contributions of the historic-geographic as well as structural schools are of great usefulness in charting and classifying the variety of narratives and texts that fall under the rubric of the fairy tale. Then we are left with the ticklish business of interpreting the meaning of these tales for their audiences. As the survey indicates, there are many ways to approach this issue, but the multiplicity of perspectives should not discourage us from, nor can we use it as an excuse to eschew, undertaking an analytical assessment of the potential significance of these stories. These narratives are too rich, too evocative, to look past their implicit influence on audiences and attempt to treat them as simply diversion or entertainment. Whether we read the plots, characters, motifs, and the basically symbolic style as conveying cultural values, sexist strictures, psychological proclivities, or philosophical paradigms, the point is that they are telling us something, many things, and it is incumbent upon us as audience members and as students of the fairy tale as a genre to attempt to decipher the ideas and concerns embedded in the narrative semiology of these memorable, enduring, and appealing of stories. In a way, fairy tales are the beginning of storytelling, the heart of literary communication. They are among the stories we first remember and longest retain. We can do no less than to try to understand why we enjoy them as much as we do.

Recommended Reading

Afanasyev (also Afanasiev or Afanasief), Alexander Nikolyaevich. *Russian Fairy Tales.* Trans. Norbert Guterman; illus. Alexander Alexieff. New York: Pantheon, 1973.

———. *Russian Folktales.* Trans. Natalie Duddington; illus. Dick Hart. New York: Funk & Wagnalls, 1967.

Andersen, Hans Christian. *Eighty Fairy Tales.* New York: Pantheon Books, 1976.

Andreas, Evelyn. *The Big Treasury Book of Fairy Tales.* Illus. Art Seiden. New York: Grosset & Dunlap, 1954.

Arbuthnot, May Hill. *Time for Fairy Tales; Old and New.* Illus. John Averill and others. Chicago: Scott, Foresman, 1961.

Arbuthnot, May Hill, and Mark Taylor. *Time for Old Magic.* Illus. John Averill and others. Glenview, Ill.: Scott, Foresman, 1970.

Árnason, Jon. *Islandic Legends.* Trans. G. Powell and E. Magnusson. London: Richard Bentley, 1864.

Asbjörnsen, Peter Christen, and Jörgen Moe, eds. *East of the Sun and West of the Moon.* Illus. Tom Vroman. New York: Macmillan, The Macmillan Classics, 1963. First published 1859 as *Popular Tales from the Norse,* trans. George Webbe Dasent. Reprinted as *East o' the Sun and West o' the Moon: Fifty-nine Norwegian Folktales from the Collection of Peter Christen Asbjörnsen and Jörgen Moe,* trans. George Webbe Dasent, New York: Dover, 1970.

———. *Tales of the Fjeld.* Trans. G. W. Dasent; illus. Moyr Smith. New York: Blom, 1970.

Aulnoy, Marie, Comtesse d'. *The White Cat, and Other Old French Fairy Tales.* Arranged by Rachel Field; illus. Elizabeth MacKinstry. New York: Macmillan, 1967.

Baker, Augusta, comp. *The Golden Lynx and other tales.* Illus. Johannes Troyer. Philadelphia: Lippincott, 1960.

———. *The Talking Tree: Fairy Tales from Fifteen Lands.* Illus. Johannes Troyer. Philadelphia: Lippincott, 1955.

Bannerman, Helen. *Little Black Sambo.* Illus. Helen Bannerman. Philadelphia: Lippincott, 1923.

Barbeau, Charles Marius. *The Golden Phoenix and other French-Canadian Fairy Tales.* Retold by Michael Hornyansky; illus. Arthur Price. New York: H. Z. Wolck, 1958.

Barrie, Sir James Matthew, bart. *Peter Pan.* Illus. Nora S. Unwin. New York: Scribner, 1950.

Basile, Giovanni Batiste. *Il Pentamerone: or, The Tale of Tales.* Trans. Sir Richard Burton. New York: Liveright, 1943.

Baum, L. Frank. *The Wizard of Oz.* New York: Penguin, Puffin Books, 1982.

Beaumont, Madame Leprince de. *Beauty and the Beast.* Trans. Diane Goode. Scarsdale: Bradbury Press, 1978.

Belting, Natalia. *Elves and Ellefolk: Tales of the Little People.* Illus. Gordon Laite. New York: Holt, Rinehart, & Winston, 1961.

Berger, Terry. *Black Fairy Tales.* Illus. David Omar White. New York: Atheneum, 1969.

Bhatta, Somadeva. *The Katha savit sagara; or Ocean of the Streams of Story.* Trans. C. H. Tawney. Delhi: Munshiran Manoharlal, 1968.

Boccaccio, Giovanni. *Decameron.* The John Payne translation, revised and annotated by Charles S. Singleton. Berkeley: University of California Press, 1982.

Briggs, Katherine M., and Ruth L. Tongue, eds. *Folktales of England.* Chicago: University of Chicago Press, 1965.

Brockett, Eleanor. *Burmese and Thai Fairy Tales.* Illus. Harry and Ilse Toothill. Chicago: Follet, 1967. Also published with Follet *Persian Fairy Tales* (1968) and *Turkish Fairy Tales* (1963).

Calvino, Italo. *Italian Folk Tales.* Trans. Sylvia Mulcahy; illus. Emanuele Luzzati. New York: Dent, 1975.

Campbell, J[ohn] F[rancis]. *Popular Tales of the West Highlands, Orally Collected.* Trans. J. F. Campbell. Edinburgh, 1860; repr. Detroit: Singing Tree Press, 1969.

Carroll, Lewis. *Alice's Adventures in Wonderland & Through the Looking-Glass.* Toronto: Bantam, 1981.

Carter, Angela, ed. *The Old Wives' Fairy Tale Book.* Illus. Corinna Sargood. New York: Pantheon, 1990.

Cerquand, J. F. *Légends et récits populaires du pays basque.* 4 vols. Pau: L. Ribaut, 1875.

Chase, Richard, ed. *The Jack Tales.* Illus. Berkeley Williams. New York: Houghton Mifflin, 1943.

Chodzko, Aleksander Borejko. *Fairy Tales of the Slav Peasants and Herdsmen from the French of Aleksander Chodzko.* Trans. and illus. Emily J. Harding. New York: Dodd, Mead, 1896; rprt. New York: Kraus, 1972.

Christiansen, Reider, ed. *Folktales of Norway.* Trans. Pat Shaw Iversen. Chicago: University of Chicago Press, 1964.

Clarkson, Atelia, and Gilbert B. Cross. *World Folktales: A Scribner Resource Collection.* New York: Scribner's, 1980.

Cole, Joanna, sel. and ed. *The Best Loved Folktales of the World.* Illus. Jill Karla Schwarz. Garden City, N.Y.: Doubleday, 1982.

Collodi, Carlo (pseudonym of Carlo Lorenzini). *The Adventures of Pinocchio.* Trans. Carol Della Chiesa. New York: Macmillan, 1969.

Cosquin, Emmanuel. *Contes Populaires de Lorraine.* Paris: F. Vieweg, 1887.

Cowan, James. *Fairy Folk Tales of the Maori.* New York: AMS Press, 1977.

Crane, Thomas Frederick. *Italian Popular Tales.* Boston: Houghton, Mifflin, 1885.

Crossley-Holland, Kevin, ed. *The Faber Book of Northern Folk-Tales.* Illus. Alan Howard. London: Faber & Faber, 1983.

Curtin, Jeremiah. *Fairy Tales of Eastern Europe.* Illus. George Hood. New York: M. McBride, 1949.

———. *Tales of Fairies of the Ghost World, Collected from Oral Tradition in South-western Munster.* New York: Blom, 1971.

Dalgliesh, Alice. *The Enchanted Book; Stories Selected by Alice Dalgliesh.* Illus. Concetta Cacciola. New York: Scribner's, 1947.

David, Alfred, and Mary Elizabeth Meek, comp. *The Twelve Dancing Princesses and Other Fairy Tales.* Bloomington: Indiana University Press, 1964.

Dawkins, R. M., comp. and trans. *Modern Greek Folktales.* Oxford: Clarendon, 1953.

De la Mare, Walter John. *The Three Royal Monkeys.* Illus. Mildred E. Eldridge. New York: Knopf, 1948.

Dickens, Charles. *A Christmas Carol: A Ghost Story of Christmas.* Illus. Michael Foreman. New York: Dial Books, 1983.

———. *The Magic Fishbone; Romance from the Pen of Miss Alice Rainbird, Age Seven.* Illus. Louis Slobokin. New York: Vanguard Press, 1953.

Dorson, Richard M., ed. *Folktales Told Around the World.* Chicago: University of Chicago Press, 1975.

Douglas, Sir George Brisbane. *Scottish Fairy and Folk Tales.* New York: Arno Press, 1977.

Eberhard, Wolfram. *Chinese Fairy Tales and Folk Tales.* Norwood, Penn.: Norwood Editions, 1978.

Fillmore, Parker. *The Laughing Prince: A Book of Jugoslav Fairy Tales and Folk Tales.* Illus. Jay van Everen. New York: Harcourt, Brace, 1921.

Fortier, Alcée. *Louisiana Folktales.* Boston: Houghton, Mifflin, 1895.

Griffis, William Elliott. *Swiss Fairy Tales.* New York: Thomas Y. Crowell, 1920.

Grimms, Jacob and Wilhelm. *The Complete Grimm's Fairy Tales,* trans. Margaret Hunt, rev. James Stern. New York: Pantheon Books, 1972. First published between 1812 and 1815 as *Kinder- und Hausmärchen.* An abbreviated selection of fifty tales was translated by Edgar Taylor and published in England in 1823 as *German Popular Stories.*

Halliwell, J. O. *Popular Rhymes and Nursery Tales of England.* London: Bodley Head, 1970.

Hartland, Edwin-Sidney. *English Fairy and Folk Tales.* London: W. Scott, 1890 (repr. Detroit: Singing Press, 1968).

Hatch, Mary Cottam. *Thirteen Danish Tales.* Illus. Edgun. New York: Harcourt, Brace, 1947. (Selections from Jens Christian Bay, comp., *Danish Fairy and Folk Tales,* 1899.)

Haviland, Virginia, ed. *The Fairy Tale Treasury.* Illus. Raymond Briggs. New York: Coward, 1972. Haviland edited a series of fairy tale collections, all published by Little, Brown, & Co. in Boston, which included such titles as *Favorite Fairy Tales Told in England* (1959); *Favorite Fairy Tales Told in Ireland* (1961); *Favorite Fairy Tales Told in Norway* (1961); *Favorite Fairy Tales Told in Russia* (1961); *Favorite Fairy Tales Told in Poland* (1963); *Favorite Fairy Tales Told in Scotland* (1963); *Favorite Fairy Tales Told in Spain* (1963); *Favorite Fairy Tales Told in Italy* (1965); *Favorite Fairy Tales Told in Sweden* (1966); *Favorite Fairy Tales Told in Czechoslovakia* (1966); *Favorite Fairy Tales Told in Japan* (1967); *Favorite Fairy Tales Told in Denmark* (1971); and *Favorite Fairy Tales Told in India* (1973).

———. *Selected Tales and Sketches.* New York: Holt, Rinehart, and Winston, 1970. (Includes selections from *Twice-Told Tales,* published initially in 1837.)

Hawthorne, Nathaniel. *The Marble Faun, or the Romance of Monte Beni.* Boston: Houghton, Mifflin, & Co., 1899. (First published in 1860.)

———. *Tanglewood Tales.* Illus. S. van Abbe. London: Dent, 1962. (First published in 1853.)

———. *A Wonder Book.* Illus. S. van Abbe. London: Dent, 1961. (First published in 1852.)

Hearn, Lafcadio. *Japanese Fairy Tales.* Illus. Sonia Roelter. Mt. Vernon, N.Y.: Peter Pauper Press, 1948.

Herda, Helmut. *Fairy Tales from Many Lands.* New York: Watts, 1956.

Irving, Washington. *The Sketch Book of Geoffrey Crayon, Gent.* Boston: Twayne Publishers, 1978. (First published 1819–1820.)

Iwaya, Sueo. *Japanese Fairy Tales.* Tokyo: Kokuseido Press, 1938.

Jacobs, Joseph, comp. and ed. *Celtic Fairy Tales.* Illus. John D. Batten. New York: Putnam's, 1923.

————. *English Fairy Tales.* Illus. John D. Batten. New York: Putnam's, n.d. (first published in England in 1890).

————. *More English Fairy Tales.* Illus. John D. Batten. New York: Putnam's, n.d. (first published in England in 1893).

Kaplan, Irma. *Swedish Fairy Tales, Retold in English by Irma Kaplan.* Illus. Carol Calder. London: Muller, 1957.

Kingsley, Charles. *The Water Babies.* Illus. Harold Jones. New York: F. Watts, 1961. (First published in 1863.)

Lang, Andrew, coll. and ed. *Arabian Nights.* Illus. Vera Bock. New York: Longmans, 1951.

————. *The Blue Fairy Book.* Illus. Ben Kutcher. New York: Longman's, Green, & Co., 1948. (First published in London by Longman's in 1889.)

————. *The Crimson Fairy Tale Book.* Illus. Ben Kutcher. New York: David McKay Pub., 1962.

————. *Fifty Favorite Fairy Tales Chosen from the Color Fairy Books of Andrew Lang.* Ed. Kathleen Lines; illus. Margery Gill. New York: F. Watts, A Nonesuch Cygnet, 1964.

————. *The Green Fairy Tale Book.* Illus. Dorothy Lake Gregory. New York: Longman's, Green, 1948.

————. *The Lilac Fairy Tale Book.* Illus. H. J. Ford. New York: Dover Publications, 1968.

————. *The Olive Fairy Tale Book.* Illus. Anne Vaughan. New York: Longman's, Green, 1949.

————. *The Orange Fairy Tale Book.* Illus. Christine Price. New York: Longman's, Green, 1949.

————. *The Red Fairy Tale Book.* Illus. Marc Simont. New York: Longman's, Green, 1948.

————. *The Rose Fairy Tale Book.* Illus. Vera Bock. New York: Longman's, Green 1961.

————. *The Violet Fairy Tale Book.* Illus. Dorothy Lake Gregory. New York: Longman's, Green, 1962.

————. *The Yellow Fairy Tale Book.* Illus. Janice Holland. New York: Longman's, Green, 1948.

Langton, Jane. *The Hedgehog Boy: A Latvian Folktale, Retold by Jane Langton.* Illus. Ilse Plume. New York: Harper & Row, 1985.

Le Guin, Ursula K. *A Wizard of Earthsea.* Illus. Ruth Robbin. Berkeley: Parnassus Press, 1968.

L'Engle, Madelaine. *A Wrinkle in Time.* New York: Ariel Books, 1962.

Lewis, Clive Staples. *The Lion, the Witch, and the Wardrobe.* Illus. Pauline Burgess. New York: Macmillan, 1958.

————. *The Magician's Nephew.* Illus. Pauline Baynes. London: Bodley Head, 1955.

————. *Prince Caspian, the Return to Narnia.* Illus. Pauline Burgess. New York: Macmillan, 1951.

————. *Till We Have Faces: A Myth Retold.* New York: Harcourt, Brace, 1957.

————. *The Voyage of the Dawn Treader.* Illus. Pauline Baynes. New York: Macmillan, 1952.

Lofting, Hugh. *The Story of Dr. Dolittle, Being the History of His Peculiar Life at Home and Astonishing Adventures in Foreign Parts.* Philadelphia: Lippincott, 1948.

The Mabinogian. Trans. Geoffrey Gantz. New York: Penguin, 1976.

MacDonald, George. *At the Back of the North Wind.* Illus. Jessie Willcox Smith. Philadelphia: D. McKay, 1919.

————. *The Light Princess.* Illus. Maurice Sendak. New York: Ferrar, Straus, & Giroux, 1969.

————. *The Princess and Curdie.* Illus. Norma S. Unwin. New York: Macmillan, 1954.

————. *The Princess and the Goblin* (1871). Illus. Jessie Wilcox Smith. New York: W. Morrow, 1986.

MacLeod, Ann. *English Fairy Tales.* Illus. Ota Janecek. London: Paul Hamlyn, 1968.

MacManus, Seumas. *Donegal Fairy Stories.* Collected and told by Seumas MacManus. New York: McClure & Phillips, 1900.

Manning-Sanders, Ruth. *A Book of Dwarfs.* Illus. Robin Jacques. New York: Dutton, 1965. Followed by *A Book of Dragons* (1965); *A Book of Giants* (1965); and *A Book of Magic Animals* (1975), all illustrated by Robin Jacques and published by Dutton.

————. *The Glass Man and the Golden Bird: Hungarian Folk and Fairy Tales.* Illus. Victor G. Ambros. New York: Roy Publishers, 1968.

————. *Jonnikan and the Flying Basket: French Folk and Fairy Tales.* Illus. Victor G. Ambros. New York: Dutton, 1969.

————. *Peter and the Piskies: Cornish Folk and Fairy Tales.* Illus. Rayman Briggs. New York: Roy Publishers, 1968.

Mehdevi, Anne (Sinclair). *Persian Folk and Fairy Tales.* Illus. Paul E. Kennedy. New York: Knopf, 1965.

Milne, Alan Alexander. *The House at Pooh Corner.* Illus. Ernest H. Shepard. New York: Dutton, 1928.

————. *Winnie-the-Pooh.* Illus. Ernest H. Shepard. New York: Dutton, 1926.

Minard, Rosemary, ed. *Womenfolk and Fairy Tales.* Illus. Suzanna Klein. Boston: Houghton Mifflin, 1975.

Montrose, Anne. *The Winter Flower and Other Fairy Stories.* Illus. Mircea Vasiliu. New York: Viking Press, 1964.

Nesbit, Edith (pen name of Edith Bland). *The Complete Book of Dragons.* Illus. Erik Blegvad. New York: Macmillan, 1973.

————. *Five Children and It*. London: Benn, 1902 (repr. 1978).

————. *The Magic World*. Illus. H. R. Millar and Spencer Pryse. London: Macmillan, 1980.

Newbery, John. *A Little Pretty Pocket-book*. A facsimile edition with an introductory essay and bibliography by M. F. Thwaite. New York: Harcourt, Brace, 1967.

Norton, Mary. *Bed-Knob and Broomstick*. Illus. Erik Blegvad. New York: Harcourt, Brace, 1957.

————. *The Borrowers*. Illus. Beth and Joe Krush. New York: Harcourt, Brace, 1953. Followed by *The Borrowers Afield* (1955) and *The Borrowers Afloat* (1959), same illustrator and publisher.

Nyblom, Helena Augusta. *The Witch of the Woods; Fairy Tales from Sweden*. Illus. Nils Christian Hald. New York: Knopf, 1968.

The Ocean of Story (see Somadeva Bhatta).

Olenius, Elna. *Great Swedish Fairy Tales*. Trans. Holger Lundbergh; illus. John Bauer. New York: Delacorte Press, 1973.

Opie, Iona, and Peter Opie. *The Classic Fairy Tales*. Oxford: Oxford University Press, 1974.

Ozaki, Yei Theodora, comp. *Japanese Fairy Book*. New York: Dover Publications, 1967.

Panchatantra, trans. Arthur W. Ryder. Chicago: University of Chicago Press, 1925.

Payne, Joan Balfour. *The Raven and Other Fairy Tales*. Retold and illus. by Joan Balfour Payne. New York: Hastings House, 1969.

Perrault, Charles. *Perrault's Complete Fairy Tales* (original title, *Contes du Ma Mère L'Oye; Histoires ou Contes du Temps Passé; avec des Moralités*). Trans. A. E. Johnson and others; illus. W. Heath Robinson. New York: Dodd, Mead, 1961 (first published in France in 1697).

Pickard, Barbara Leonie. *French Legends, Tales, and Fairy Tales*. Illus. Joan Kiddell-Monroe. London: Oxford University Press, 1953.

Pyle, Howard. *Pepper and Salt; or, Seasoning for Young Folk*. New York: Harper Bros., 1913.

————. *Twilight Land*. Illus. Howard Pyle. New York: Dover Publications, 1968.

Rackham, Arthur, comp. *Arthur Rackham Fairy Book: A Book of Old Favorites with New Illustrations*. Philadelphia: Lippincott, 1930.

————, comp. and illus. *Fairy Tales from Many Lands*. New York: Viking, 1974.

Ranke, Kurt. *Folktales of Germany*. Chicago: University of Chicago Press, 1966.

Ransome, Arthur. *Old Peter's Russian Tales*. Illus. Dmitri Mitrokhim. New York: Dover Publications, 1969.

Reed, Alexander Wyclif. *Fairy Tales from the Pacific Islands*. Illus. Stewart Irwin. London: Frederick Muller, 1969.

Reeves, James. *English Fables and Fairy Stories*. Illus. Joan Kiddell-Monroe. London: Oxford University Press, 1955.

Romskaug, Brenda, comp. *Norweigian Fairy Tales*. Trans. Brenda and Reider Romskaug; illus. Ivar Pettersen. London: London University Press, 1961.

Ruskin, John. *The King of the Golden River*. Illus. Arthur Rackham. Philadelphia: Lippincott, n.d.

Saint-Exupéry, Antoine de. *The Little Prince*. Trans. Katherine Woods. New York: Reynal & Hitchcock, 1943.

Schwartz, Howard. *Elijah's Violin and Other Jewish Fairy Tales*. Illus. Linda Heller. New York: Harper & Row, 1985.

Sebillot, Paul. *Contes populaires de las Haute-Bretagne*. Paris: Maisonneuve, 1882.

Sendak, Maurice. *Where the Wild Things Are*. New York: Harper and Row, 1984.

Seuss, Dr. (Theodore Geisel). *The Cat in the Hat*. New York: Random House, 1957.

Southey, Robert. "The Story of the Three Bears," in *The Doctor*. Ed. J. W. Warter. London: Dent, 1849.

Stephens, James. *Irish Fairy Tales*. Illus. Arthur Rackham. New York: Macmillan, 1920.

Steptoe, John. *Mufaro's Beautiful Daughters: an African Tale*. New York: Lothrop and Shepard Books, 1987.

Straparola, Giovanni Francesco. *The Facetious Nights (Le piacevoli notti*, also known as *The Pleasureful Nights* or *The Pleasant Nights)*. Trans. W. G. Waters. London: Society of Bibliophiles, 1898.

Tezel, Naki. *Fairy Tales from Turkey*. Trans. Margery Kent; illus. Olga Lehmann. London: Routledge & Kegan Paul, 1951.

Thackeray, William Makepeace. *The Rose and the Ring*, or, *The History of Prince Giglio and Prince Bulbo; A Fireside Pantomine for Great and Small Children*. Illus. William M. Thackeray, John Gilbert, and Paul Hogarth. New York: Dutton, 1963.

Thompson, Stith. *One Hundred Favorite Folktales*. Illus. Franz Altschuler. Bloomington: Indiana University Press, 1968.

Thorpe, Benjamin, comp. *Tales on the North Wind, Old Fairy Tales Retold by Benjamin Thorpe and Thomas Keightley*. New York: Roy Publishers, 1956.

Told Under the Green Umbrella: Old Stories for New Children. Edited by the Association for Childhood Education, Literature Committee. New York: Macmillan, 1962.

Tolkien, J. R. R. *The Hobbit*. New York: Ballantine Books, 1966.

———. *The Lord of the Rings*. New York: Ballantine Books, 1965.

Travers, P. L. *Mary Poppins*. Illus. Mary Shepard. New York: Harcourt, Brace, 1934.

Turnbull, E. Lucia. *Fairy Tales of India*. Illus. Hazel Cook. New York: Criterion Books, 1960.

White, E. B. *Charlotte's Web*. Illus. Garth Williams. New York: Harper, 1952.

———. *Stuart Little*. Illus. Garth Williams. New York: Harper, 1973.

White, Terence Hanbury. *The Once and Future King*. New York: Putnam, 1958. The first book, which has the greatest fairy tale influence, was published on its own as *The Sword in the Stone*. New York: Putnam's, 1939.

Whitney, Thomas P. *In a Certain Kingdom; Twelve Russian Fairy Tales*. Trans. Thomas Whitney; illus. Dieter Lange. New York: Macmillan, 1972.

———, ed. and trans. *Vasilisa the Beautiful*. Illus. Nancy Hogrogian. New York: Macmillan, 1970.

Whittier, John Greenleaf. *The Supernaturalism of New England*. Norman: University of Oklahoma Press, 1969. (First published in 1847.)

Wiggin, Kate Douglas, and Nora Archibald Smith, eds. *The Fairy Ring*. Illus. Warren Chappell. New York: Doubleday, 1967.

Wilde, Oscar. *The Happy Prince and Other Fairy Stories*. New York: Putnam, 1912.

Williams, Margery (pen name of Margery Williams Bianco). *The Velveteen Rabbit, or How Toys Become Real*. Illus. William Nicholson. Garden City, N.Y.: Doubleday, n.d.

Wilson, Barbara Ker. *Fairy Tales of France*. Illus. William McLaren. New York: Dutton, 1960.

———. *Fairy Tales of Germany*. Illus. Gertrude Mittelmann. New York: Dutton, 1959.

———. *Fairy Tales of India*. Illus. Rene Mackensie. New York: Dutton, 1960.

———. *Fairy Tales of Ireland*. Illus. G. W. Muller. New York: Dutton, 1959.

———. *Fairy Tales of Persia*. Illus. G. W. Muller. New York: Dutton, 1961.

Yeats, William Butler. *Fairy and Folk Tales of Ireland*. New York: Macmillan, 1973. (First published in 1892.)

Yolen, Jane. *The Moon Ribbon, and Other Tales*. Illus. David Palladini. New York: Crowell, 1976.

Zheleznova, Irina L'vovna. *Folk Tales of Russian Lands*. Trans. Irina Zheleznova. New York: Dover Publications, 1969.

Ziner, Feenie. *Cricket Boy: A Chinese Tale*. Illus. Ed Young. Garden City, N.Y.: Doubleday, 1977.

Zipes, Jack, ed. *Don't Bet on the Prince: Contemporary Feminist Fairy Tales in North America and England*. New York: Methuen, 1986.

———. *Spells of Enchantment: The Wondrous Fairy Tales of Western Culture*. New York: Viking Press, 1992.

Index

About the Author

Steven Swann Jones is Professor of English at California State University, Los Angeles. He received his doctorate in English and Folklore from the University of California, Davis in 1979. He has published essays on fairy tales in *Fabula; Journal of American Folklore; Research in African Literatures; Western Folklore; Southern Folklore;* and *The Journal of Folklore Research.* He coedited a volume of *Papers in Comparative Studies* ("Directions in Folklore Research," vol. 2 [1982–83], and is coeditor of volume 52 (January 1993, No. 1) of *Western Folklore* on "Perspectives on the Innocent Persecuted Heroine in Fairy Tales." He has previously authored *Folklore and Literature in the United States: An Annotated Bibliography of Studies of Folklore in American Literature* (New York: Garland, 1984) and *The New Comparative Method: Structural and Symbolic Analysis of the Allomotifs of "Snow White"* (FF Communications No. 247, Helsinki: Academia Scientiarum Fennica, 1990). He is currently president of the California Folklore Society.